FAUST

Johann Wolfgang von Goethe
FAUST
A tragedy • Parts One and Two
translated in a
performing version by
Robert David MacDonald

OBERON BOOKS
LONDON

First published in this translation in 1988 by Oberon Books Ltd. (incorporating Absolute Classics)
521 Caledonian Road, London N7 9RH
Tel: 020 7607 3637 / Fax: 020 7607 3629
e-mail: oberon.books@btinternet.com
www.oberonbooks.com

Reprinted in this edition with revisions in 2002

A catalogue record for this book is available from the British Library.

ISBN: 1 870259 11 4

Cover design: Andrzej Klimowski

Typography: Jeff Willis

Proofread by Prufrock – www.prufrock.co.uk

Printed in Great Britain by Antony Rowe Ltd, Chippenham.

for Roy Marsden

Contents

Introduction

The origins of this translation are somewhat disordered. It sprang first from a suggestion of Dr Georg Heuser, then director of the Goethe-Institut in Glasgow, which had helped to fund several productions at the Citizens' Theatre, including Goethe's *Torquato Tasso,* a lone salute in the British theatre to the 150th anniversary of the author's death. After the Citizens' had mounted Karl Kraus's monumental *The Last Days of Mankind* at the Edinburgh Festival in 1983, *Faust* seemed a natural step to take in the direction of staging plays normally considered unperformable.

Two years later, in November 1985, the Citizens' Company performed a version of both parts of the play on one evening. It is that version which is the basis of this translation, or rather, the present translation was used as a basis for that production. It was clear that the initial problem was one of selection. The first intention was to perform the play over two evenings, with marathon performances of both parts at weekends; for various reasons, some fairly mundane, it was decided to try to stage the whole play, or as much of it as was feasible, on one evening. Not the least of these reasons was the feeling that the numberless inconsistencies between the two parts of the tragedy could most easily be reconciled if placed within the limits of a single evening in the theatre.

This made it necessary to cut roughly half of the translation as it stood, and to re-order the remainder to suit the available resources, material, financial and human, as well as the production which was envisaged. This done, it hit the stage, with considerable success, on 8 November 1985.

And there the matter rested for some eighteen months, until the Lyric Theatre, Hammersmith decided to present the play, under the direction of David Freeman, with a company led by Simon Callow, who had long been interested in playing one (or both?) of the two leads. This time, it was definitely to be on two evenings, of approximately three and a half hours apiece, and David Freeman was anxious to incorporate a considerable amount of new material, emphasising certain aspects of the play, in particular Faust's striving after the secrets of the alchemists, and his feeling of kinship with Nature as a force of creation. In addition, Nigel Osborne was to write music for the production, which meant restoring much of the lyric element, largely neglected in Glasgow. Lastly, the Glasgow company, twenty strong, had not doubled parts – the roles were all concertinaed and adapted so as to be played as single roles all the way through the play. This gave a certain much-needed consistency to the material, but involved some wrenching of the cloth to fit the dummy. David Freeman, choosing to work with a smaller company of twelve, over a wider time-span, was not up against that particular problem, although, with *Faust,* a problem solved, or at any rate shelved, is apt to produce ten others, like armed men from dragons' teeth. (Rather than confuse the reader with conflicting directions from both productions, I have restored Goethe's speech-ascriptions here. The reader will have however to be fairly alert, as Goethe tends to reserve his stage directions for the more sensational moments – 'He changes himself into a giant tortoise' or 'She bursts into flame and shoots into the air' – rather than such mundane goings-on as 'Enter so-and-so'.)

From this rather circumstantial account it is clear that the main preoccupation when translating and adapting *Faust* for the theatre is one of imparting consistency to a whole which may appear inchoate. Emerson may have been right to say that 'a foolish consistency is the hobgoblin of little minds... with consistency a great soul has nothing to do', but those lesser souls who sit in theatres like the evening to hang together in some sort or other. David Luke, in his admirable introduction to the most recent, and best, complete translation (World's Classics, OUP, 1987–94), points out that Faust studies divide into two schools, the historical or genetic, which seeks to emphasise the discrepancies as being part of Goethe's continual development over the very long time it took to write *Faust,* and the unitarian, which insists that the whole work must be regarded as an integrated whole, springing from a single, unchanging conception, to be imposed on it at all costs. It would be good to avoid the lunacies of either of these two schools, but it must be said that while it is desirable to face the specifically theatrical problem as a unitarian, it is also mandatory to remember that the play was written, over a period of more than half a century, by the most enquiring mind in Europe during those sixty-odd years, whose own comments stress the fragmentariness of the work, but who, we must believe, built the later parts of the great structure on the basis of what he had already published. Since the time between his beginning and ending the play is exactly equivalent to that between man's first powered flight at Kitty Hawk, and the first man-made orbit of the earth in space, it might be useful, at this point, to give a timetable summarising the main stages and periods of composition, along with one or two historical facts which bear on the matter, or are simply interesting in themselves. (The figures in brackets after the dates indicate Goethe's age at the time.)

1749 28 August: Goethe born in Frankfurt am Main.

1756 Birth of Mozart.

FIRST PERIOD: 1768–1775 (19–26)

1768 (19) Faust play, a popular corruption of Marlowe, with folk additions, performed in Frankfurt, where Goethe would have seen it.

1772 (23) January 14: execution in Frankfurt of Susanna Margaretha (i.e. Gretchen) Brandt for the murder of her illegitimate baby.

Probable date of beginning work on the earliest version of the play, the so-called *Urfaust*. Prose scenes: Faust and Mephistopheles (Gloomy day – open country), and Prison.

1772–73 (23–24) Winter: numerous notes made for a full-scale draft of certain scenes: Introductory monologue, Earth-Spirit, Faust-Wagner, Mephistopheles-Student.

1773 (24) Publication of his first play, *Goetz von Berlichingen.*

1773–75 (24–26) Composition of the remainder of *Urfaust*, which remained unpublished until 1887, when a manuscript transcript was discovered. It contains at least the germs of most of the scenes eventually incorporated in Part One, the greatest gaps being the walk outside the city gate, the summoning by Faust of Mephistopheles, and the Walpurgis Night scenes.

1775–86 (26–37) Goethe meets and becomes engaged to Lili Schoenemann, but breaks off the engagement after a few months. He enters the service of the Grand Duke of Weimar, later obtaining the post of Minister for War and Roadworks. Meets Charlotte von Stein, with whom he corresponds over a long period, and who inspires a great deal of his poetry.

1776 (27) American Declaration of Independence.

SECOND PERIOD: 1788–1790 (39–41)

1788 (39) February: resumes work on *Faust,* after completion of work on *Egmont,* and the early versions of *Iphigenie* and *Tasso.*

Beginning of his liaison with Christiane Vulpius, whom he married in 1806 (57), and by whom he had five children, of whom only August, born 1789, survived.

March: travels in Italy, plan for *Faust.* Witch's kitchen, Forest and Cave, Auerbach's Cellar (verse version).

1789 (40) Outbreak of French Revolution.

1790 (41) Publication of *Faust, A Fragment,* the second stage of the composition: it arouses little interest publicly. Like its forerunner, it omits the wager between Faust and Mephistopheles, and stops short after the Cathedral scene.

1791 (42) Death of Mozart (35). Birth of Meyerbeer. Goethe later says Mozart would have been the ideal composer for *Faust,* then spoils it by adding that Meyerbeer might be able to do it, 'except it would never occur to him'.

1793 (44) Beheading of Louis XVI and Marie-Antoinette.

1797(48) Birth of Schubert.

THIRD PERIOD: 1797–1801 (48–52)

1797 (48) 22 June: to Schiller, '…I have decided to go to work on my Faust.' Schiller points out the inconsistencies between the various fragments of the work. The Prologue in Heaven becomes the frame of the piece.

23 June: extensive plan for *Faust* Part One.

24 June: *Dedication.* Also, probably the *Valediction* intended for the end of the play, but which in the end Goethe does not publish.

1797–1801 (48–52) Prelude – On the Stage, Prologue – In Heaven, Night (completed). Before the City Gate, Faust's Study, Walpurgis Night, Valentine's Death, Prison (verse version). Certain scenes from Act Five of Part Two.

1800 (51) *Helen in the Middle Ages, Satyr-play* (written as a separate work, but later incorporated into Act Three of Part Two).

1804 (55) Napoleon Emperor of France.

1805 (56) Death of Schiller.

1806 (57) Battle of Jena, delays publication of *Part One.*

1808 (59) Publication of *Faust, The First Part of the Tragedy.*

1810 (61) A production of Part One is planned in Weimar, but comes to nothing.

1816 (67) Plan for Part Two drawn up for Goethe's autobiography, *Poetry and Truth.*

FOURTH PERIOD: 1825–1831 (76–82)

1825–31 (76–82) Act Five.

1825 (76) Act Three (Helen).

1826 (77) Spring: Act Five, The Great Forecourt of the Palace. Plans for the Second Act.

1827 (78) Act Three published as: *Helena, a classical-romantic phantasmagoria. Interlude for Faust.*

1827–30 (78–81) Acts One and Two.

1828 (79) Death of Schubert (31). Sent Goethe a packet of songs, settings of words by Goethe, which he failed to open.

1829 (80) January 19: *Faust I* performed complete at the Court Theatre in Braunschweig under the direction of August Klingemann. In the same year there are further performances in Frankfurt, Bremen, Weimar and Dresden.

1831 (82) Act Four. Some scenes of Act Five, e.g. Philemon and Baucis, and the two scenes before the final scene.
22 July: 'Brought the great work to a conclusion.'

1832 (83) 22 March: Death of Goethe.
Publication of *Faust, The Second Part of the Tragedy*, as the first volume of his posthumous works. Goethe forbade the publication during his life time, possibly for fear of censorship, possibly in accordance with his principle of *'nie zu viel erklären'* (never explain too much). In 1827 (78) he said to Eckermann: 'The Germans are really extraordinary people...they come to me and ask me what ideas I have tried to incorporate in my play – as if I knew myself or could express it!' Goethe was adept at playing peek-a-boo with scholars and critics.

1854 April 4: *Faust II* performed with a heavily-cut text in the Stadttheater in Hamburg.

1876 May 6 and 7: Otto Devrient stages the first complete performances of Parts One and Two in the Court Theatre at Weimar.
First complete staging of Wagner's *Der Ring der Nibelungen* at the opening of the first Bayreuth Festival.

1887 Publication of *Urfaust*.

From this rather extensive chronology it will be clear that the play, unlike Goethe's other plays, or almost any other play by any other author, was written with neither the neatly preconceived structure, nor the concentration of subject-matter and diction, which we conventionally assume to be essential to dramatic production. On the contrary, *Faust* grew like a wood, the new growth continually changing the aspect of the whole, fertilised by, yet not necessarily obscuring, what had gone before, and full of alien, variegated, often parasitic forms of life. Since it conforms to none of the rules, it must be considered independently of any such rules. In a poem called *Leavetaking,* written for an actor to speak as Epilogue at the end of Part One, Goethe compares the poem to human life – 'it certainly has a beginning and an end, it's just that it doesn't make a whole.' The ambiguity of his feelings for a work which was clearly of great personal importance to him, but which he was continually deprecating, particularly to Schiller, without whose encouragement it would never have been completed, indicates that he never really considered the work finished, but realised that its quasi-autobiographical nature was such that its final form would be whatever stage it had reached at the time he died. His reluctance to publish Part Two, along with the reckless impracticality of the stage directions – though this last proved no obstacle to *Peter Pan* – possibly confirms this view. One could conclude, with Dr Johnson's view of the Shakespearean history play: 'as it had no plan, it had no limits.'

The implication of all this for exegetists, commentators, interpreters, and, in the field that most concerns us here, theatrical directors, is that it will always be open season on *Faust*. It is like a huge stone quarry, from which people will hew out the play that interests them at the time, still leaving behind a quarry apparently undiminished, from which others will hack away according to their needs. What is excavated may be a masterpiece, or a shambles, but the elusiveness as well as the toughness of the huge epic will absorb it all, brilliance along with ineptitude. Like *Hamlet* or America, the target is so big we are all bound to hit it somewhere.

For a translator, there are two extreme situations: first, the translation of, say, a legal or technical document on a subject such as the projected wheat-yield of the Argentine for next year – any slip made here in accuracy might have economic repercussions of the most disastrous kind, but no one will blame you if accuracy is achieved at the cost of limpidity of prose; secondly, at the other extreme, there is the translation of opera libretti, where the new text must not only fit the notes exactly, both in stress and phrasing, but should, where possible, give open vowels on high notes to grateful singers – another sort of precision, and you will be forgiven the odd attack of agreeable gibberish. In both cases, however, you are dealing with texts unlikely to be considerable works of literature. Lawyers and technicians are largely immune to, and rightly mistrustful of, evocative language, and opera libretti are, not always fairly, a standing joke. Both forms are subservient to strict requirements outwith the actual task of writing: there is no reason why such works should not have distinction of language – but it does not often happen.

Between these two poles of the *craft* of translation comes imaginative literature, which combines both headaches. In the first place, a writer's choice of words is always precise – the better the writer, the less replaceable the word. Every word not anchored to an unequivocal material meaning, (e.g. *fire, yellow, blood, pencil, monocle*) is surrounded by a nimbus of associative overtones, like the harmonics of a vibrating string, based, not least of all, on the actual sound of the word, (a few to try: *doom, swig, sleek, zest, grandeur*). These overtones will almost always escape the translator, who can hope at best to convey them in the wider context of an entire passage, rather than word by word. Inaccuracy here may not threaten the economics of the Third World, but it will surely militate against the acceptance, accessibility and circulation of the author's work.

Nor is the operatic headache wholly absent: every prose sentence should have a rhythm as taut as a line of verse, any significant extension of which will make the sentence sag. Translations, in their attempts to convey precision of meaning, nearly always end up slightly longer than their originals, but the perils of this should be kept in mind, and nowhere more than in dramatic dialogue, where pace and characterisation depend largely on the rhythm of the sentences.

If prose lays obligations on its translators, verse, to come to the point at last, has even stricter laws, although their mere existence, by restricting the problem of choice, makes some things superficially easier: a diminution of liberty means a lessening of responsibility, like living in a police state. The problem of length, for one, vanishes: fifty lines of verse translate into fifty lines of verse, and that is that. The rhythmic dynamics are laid down: iambic pentameter, alexandrine, heroic couplet, limerick. Much as consecutive performances of an opera will not differ in length by more than a minute or two, while those of a play can differ by as much as ten minutes from one evening to another, so the translation of a verse play need not, nor should it, differ in length from the original by more than a few lines.

The fact that, since the first English translation of Part One of *Faust* appeared in 1808, they have been rolling in at an average rate of one every eighteen months, giving a current count of well into three figures, should make the most arrogant toiler in this particular vineyard pause a moment before inflicting yet another version on a long-suffering world. But a glance at the lugubrious and, for the most part, well-deserved fate of the previous versions will quickly show that deathlessness in the original is no guarantee that immortality will rub off on the translation. In fact, it might be no bad thing were all translations to be equipped with an auto-destruct mechanism to volatilise them after a statutory period. This is particularly so in the case of translations made specifically for the theatre: they are prepared for a particular set of circumstances, a particular set of collaborators, mutually engaged in saving each other's bacon, all united in the delicious task of putting one over on the public, at a particular time – once these conditions cease to obtain, the translation must necessarily lose some of its effectiveness. These are, admittedly, somewhat nice differences, and a translator, like any other citizen, must eat and pay school fees, while publishers like to keep their books in print for as long as they can, but the essentially transient and, indeed, voguish nature of the theatre does mean that translations go out of date quickly and easily. In the case of a film, the matter is different: we are dealing there with a work of its time, where all the elements are, as it were, frozen at the same moment. In the cinema, we applaud a mammoth in a block of ice: in the theatre we would complain that it is not an elephant. *Pro captu lectoris habent sua fata libelli* – equally, it is on the capacity of the spectator that the fate of plays, and their translations, depends.

It took an arch-romantic, Victor Hugo, to provide the most classical definition of verse – *Le vers, c'est la forme optique de la pensée* – and it is this optical form we must preserve in attempting any transposition of Goethe's complicated forms of thought. This, of course, extends into the area of rhyme. It is not always clear, to me at any rate, just why Goethe chooses the metres he does, or why he chooses to go in and out of rhyme at any given moment, but the fact that he does so seems reason enough to follow him, even if the irregularity of his use of any particular form may give us a certain freedom in doing so.

It used to be said that the English could never translate Racine, because the six-foot rhyming alexandrine was repellent to the English tongue, which would fall almost unbidden into the iambic pentameter, as one can still see in the work of journalists writing in a hurry. The consequence was that Racine would be translated into straight, unrhymed, English blank verse, which suited him much as a saddle suits a cow, making him sound like dull Shakespeare, where a translation into alexandrines might at least have made him sound like dull Racine. In the same way, the daunting fact that Germany's greatest writer chose to write his greatest work largely in rhythms the English would regard as being more suitable for television jingles should not prevent us from attempting to preserve what is, finally, a visual expression of his thought. To abandon Goethe's rhythms, let alone his rhymes, is to prejudice accuracy from the start.

It is true that there are limits to the fidelity with which one can, or perhaps should, imitate the patterns of the original. English is comparatively poverty-stricken in feminine terminations, compared with the more heavily-inflected Slavonic and Teutonic languages, let alone Italian – and with what *Schadenfreude* the English translator of opera sees the luckless Italian librettists wrestling with a full close on an accented beat. Feminine rhymes are even more of a problem, unless one is to have defeatist recourse to the '-ation' repertoire. In addition, the necessity of rhyming every four beats or, often, by the time we reach the final scene of Part Two, every two beats, can put a strain on the versifier to a point where one begins to tinker with the sense to fit the rhyme.

Here we come up against the problem which David Luke has aptly called 'the cost of rhyme': how much we can afford to lose precision of thought to the advantage of fidelity to form. These things are bound to be a matter of personal taste, and in this version I have preferred to keep the meaning clear, since it was designed to be heard rather than read, at the cost of committing what seemed to me more venial sins against prosody. To follow Goethe's metre- and rhyme-schemes, even to ending lines with the same word as the German, as Walter Arndt (1976) did, however skilfully, seems to me to impose fidelity on oneself more as a moral duty than a pleasure; a translation is necessarily a love affair, sometimes unrequited, between an author and an admirer, and while it may not always end in marriage, equally, not all infidelities end in the divorce courts, and there is no virtue in monogamy simply because one is frightened of catching something. On the other hand, when Goethe embarks on a set-piece based on the alternation of masculine and feminine endings, as, for example, the elegy on Byron after the death of Euphorion in Part Two, and the greater part of the last scene of all, it seems to me that to ignore this pattern is to remove the mainspring from the verse, and let it fall into a sort of amiable jog-trot, fatal in the theatre.

Although Goethe, with a larger armoury of rhymes at his disposal, hardly ever uses ones regarded in German as impure – though *selig/froehlich* grates on the English ear, and *treu/frei* has always sounded rather yokelish to me – I admit to having been rather less fussy, and included rhymes from Scotland (*cairn/discern, prudent/shouldn't*) to Sloane Square (*ground/mined, forced/lost*), along with the dropped ending (*invitation/creation' ['s]*), and the overlap to the following line (*serious/criteria s[-aying]*), as well as what I would call 'bagpipe rhymes' after MacNeice's poem where nothing actually rhymes, but everything seems to (*fastness/mistress, hoist/most, estate/complete*). I have also taken advantage of the sloppiness of English speech, which allows words such as *tire, power, ordinary, science, different,* to gain or lose a syllable at discretion.

It is always possible for a reader to re-read, and for an actor to rehearse, a passage, but for a spectator, receiving simultaneous aural and visual impressions, there is no second chance. I was all the time aware that I was dealing with spoken dialogue, and while this obliged me to make sure that the lines were both speakable and intelligible, it also lent a certain freedom to use rhymes I would normally fight shy of: I find it harder to accept the English Received Pronunciation rhyme of *fair/here*, than I do the straight sight-rhyme *owned/crowned*, and a couplet such as:

> A lust for glory? It is plain to see
> that you've been keeping heroines' company.

is, frankly, excusable only on grounds that the line is meant to be mildly funny. However, to quote Emerson once more: 'When skating over thin ice, our safety lies in our speed', and I know that whereas readers always read at about the consistent same speed, accomplished actors perform with an endlessly varied range of speed and volume, qualities on which I have gratefully relied.

So much then for what one may call the look of the thing. It was also, however, particularly important, if the actors were to be as grateful to me as I to them, that they had accessible lines to say. Goethe's misfortune, as far as his English translations were concerned, was to write at a time when the English theatre was at its nadir. Whenever there is a period with no individual style, people will hark back to the last period *but one* when there *was* a marked style. The English theatre of the nineteenth century could find nothing better to do than try to revive the glories of the Elizabethan drama, a desperate trend which spawned an infinity of infinitely tedious pieces in pseudo-Jacobethan English, and which, after seducing nearly every major poet into wasting his time, finally petered out at the beginning of the twentieth century with the plays of Stephen Phillipps, whose *Faust* appeared, and apparently disappeared, in 1908. Now Goethe's German, even at its most statuesque and 'classical', is in no way archaic, and, while avoiding the cuter modernisms, which could send the translation out of date before opening night, I have tried to maintain a natural word-order, with a vocabulary to match, and to skirt round the more tortuous gyrations of 'poetic' diction of the kind practised by Anna Swanwick, LL.D., in 1850:

Rubbish, in thousand shapes, may I not call
What in this moth-world doth my being bound?

Indeed, Dr Swanwick, that is exactly what you may call it.
A further preoccupation in preparing a practical, performing
script of the play was the need to marry up the two parts, so
different in conception and indeed in diction, so that they
seemed to hang together more closely than they in fact do.
Here the Devil became, for once, the saviour. Faust himself
changes markedly between the two parts, Mephistopheles
scarcely at all – hardly surprising since it is Faust's character
which develops, the Devil's being, by definition, already
formed – even when he is finally, albeit briefly, thrown off
balance by what H C Earwicker called the 'fleshasplush
cushionettes of some chubby boybold love of an angel'. It was
necessary, all the same, to bring some of the more ironic tone
– not a common quality in German literature – of Part Two
over into Part One. The man who betrays Gretchen must be
the same man who ends up draining the marshes: the Gretchen
tragedy must be seen as the first, if the decisive, episode in a
series of trials, and not as a separate play which, thanks to
Gounod, it often becomes. It is the supreme irony of the play
that the great scientist, when faced with infinite choice, chooses
a love affair which he conducts with all the egotistical
inefficiency of an adolescent. When he has finally destroyed
the object of his love, he proceeds, like many people who give
up in that field – compare Alberich in Wagner's *Ring* – to the
exercise of other less attractive passions: money, power, war,
and organising other people's lives.

Sight, sound and sense: what does it look like, what does it
sound like, and what does it mean? These are the three criteria
by which a translation, 'the art of the least intolerable
sacrifice…the instinctive choice between competing
imperfections' (Luke), must be measured against its original.
In the case of an adaptation, such as this, one is laying oneself
open to further attack, and not only from those purists for
whom the least divagation is tantamount to handing the book
over to the public hangman for burning in the market place.

Although this version is an amalgamation of two separate and very different productions, restoring the cuts made in both – it seemed a shame to waste what had taken some trouble to do – the main omissions caused no argument.

Apart from the 'torture of a thousand cuts', minute, and less minute, excisions, varying in length from a single word to over a hundred lines in every scene that was preserved – and it is surprising what the removal of the words 'that' and 'very', and the dropping of similes will do for the athleticism of style – nearly all the major omissions are there, or rather not there, to keep the story of Faust himself before the spectator. It is as surprising as it is clear how the purely dramatic interest of the play falls away when he is not on the stage: even Mephistopheles, a far showier part, cannot sustain the interest *on his own.* The main total or near-total casualties were the Student/Baccalaureus, a lot of the Walpurgis Night, the whole of the Walpurgis Night's Dream Intermezzo (except for the last four lines), the Carnival at the Emperor's Palace in Part Two, huge chunks of the Classical Walpurgis Night, the scene of the Emperor after the battle and, of course, quantities of the final scene. To say 'of course' about the excision of what must be the supreme poetic achievement of a world-language sounds frivolous, but in the context of any production, the treatment of the final scene will be a sort of shorthand summing-up of the aims and ideals of the production itself and, as such, cannot be over-extended without becoming over-emphatic and repetitive, telling the audience something they should already have a fair inkling of after all the time they have spent in the theatre. In production, I originally transposed the scenes in Auerbach's cellar and the witch's kitchen, as it seemed that the natural break should come between leaving the study and entering the world, and that Faust's rejuvenation was the best bridge between the two levels. For publication, Goethe's scene-order is restored. Before the birth of Euphorion, I have introduced a monologue for Mephistopheles, culled, as are several other less important and less noticeable lardings, from Goethe's early rejected sketches. This was partly to defuse the rather high-falutin' tone that begins to be established by the love scene of Faust and Helen, and which, if carried over unbroken into the Euphorion scene would be, I felt, for British audiences at any rate, unendurably po-faced: it also had the real practical advantage of conveying the not entirely clear narrative in very few but vivid lines.

Two last points: the alert reader will notice a sprinkling of quotations in the text, some hardly available to Goethe, and very few of them actually justified by the original text. Goethe, like many cultivated men, thought quotation was one of the Masonic handshakes by which kindred spirits recognised one another, and, where it seemed an adequate translation of the line, I have not hesitated to suggest something which may cause a tingle of recognition and, perhaps for a moment, make a spectator forget he is watching a translation. Finally, in the scene 'Gloomy day – open country', the only scene which Goethe left in prose when he finally revised Part One (the succeeding scene could arguably be said to be in verse, of a kind), I was in two minds, whether to assume Goethe had his own good reasons for leaving it as it was and, on the other hand, wondering whether it might not be better brought in line with the rest of the play, and worked in verse. The solution to this impasse was a mixture of the cunning and the crass, and should appeal to all connoisseurs of the British art of compromise.

Other sins will be revealed to superficial study, and for those may the spirit of Sir Thomas Urquhart, the translator of Rabelais, intercede for me, to allow the translation to stand on its own two feet, as a tribute of gratitude for the time spent in the company of its original, remembering always the warning of Vladimir Nabokov:

What is translation? On a platter
A poet's pale and glaring head:
A parrot's screech, a monkey's chatter,
And profanation of the dead.

RDM
Glasgow, 1988

Characters

DIRECTOR	LIESCHEN
AUTHOR	VALENTINE
ACTOR	CHOIR
RAPHAEL	WILL-O'-THE-WISP
GABRIEL	WITCHES
MICHAEL	WARLOCKS
ARCHANGELS	HALF-WITCH
MEPHISTOPHELES	GENERAL
GOD	MINISTER
FAUST	PARVENOO
EARTH-SPIRIT	An AUTHOR
WAGNER	HUCKSTER-WITCH
STUDENT	ARIEL
GIRLS	EMPEROR
CITIZENS	COURTIERS
OLD WOMAN	CHANCELLOR
SOLDIERS	TREASURER
OLD MAN	STEWARD
SPIRITS CHORUS	ASTROLOGER
BRANDER	DRUNKARD
CHORUS	FEAR
FROSCH	HOPE
SIEBEL	PRUDENCE
ALTMEYER	BOY CHARIOTEER
TUTTI	PLUTUS
HE-MONKEY	WOMEN
WITCH	HERALD
GRETCHEN	AVARICE
MARTHA	CHORUS of NYMPHS

FOOL
CHAMBERLAIN
BLONDE
BRUNETTE
LADY
PAGE
ARCHITECHT
PROFESSOR
HOMUNCULUS
SPHINXES
SIRENS
CHIRON
MANTO
LAMIAE
EMPUSA
ANAXAGORAS
THALES
DRYAD
PHORKYADS
PROTEUS
NEREUS
GALATEA
HELEN
PHORKYAS
PENTHALIS
LYNCEUS
EUPHORION
WHACKER
SACKER

PACKER
SCOUTS
STACKER
ARCHBISHOP
GUARD
WANDERER
BAUCIS
PHILEMON
WANT
NEED
DEBT
CARE
ZOMBIES
HOST OF HEAVEN
ANGELS
PATER ECSTATICUS
PATER PROFUNDUS
PATER SERAPHICUS
CHORUS of the BLESSED
BOYS
DOCTOR MARIANUS
CHORUS of PENITENT
WOMEN
MAGNA PECCATRIX
MULIER SAMARITANA
MARIA AEGYPTIACA
THE PENINTENT
MATER GLORIOSA
CHORUS MYSTICUS

The original version of this translation was made for and first performed by the Citizens Company, Glasgow, at the Citizens' Theatre, Glasgow, on 8 November 1985 with the following cast:

DIRECTOR, Giles Havergal

AUTHOR, Harry Gibson

ANGELS and MINISTERS:

  of Finance, Derwent Watson

  of State, Ciaran Hinds

  of War, Patrick Hannaway

  of Religion, John Somerville

FAUST, Mark Lewis

MEPHISTO, Andrew Wilde

PRINCE, later EMPEROR, Rupert Farley

GRETCHEN, Yolanda Vasquez

HELEN, Julia Blalock

MARTHA, Ida Schuster

WITCH, Roberta Taylor

WAGNER, Robin Sneller

VALENTINE, Jonathan Coyne

EUPHORION, John Wagland

with John Ferry, Derek Fraser, Hugh Shiels

Director, Robert David MacDonald

Design, Kenny Miller

Lighting Design, Gerry Jenkinson

Assistant Director, Paul Elkins

This somewhat revised version was subsequently first performed at the Lyric Theatre, Hammersmith, London, on 28 March 1988, with the following cast:

Simon Callow, as FAUST

Peter Lindford, as MEPHISTO

and

Caroline Bliss

Paul Brightwell

Toby Davies

Jack Ellis

Linda Kerr Scott

Robyn Moore

Andy Serkis

Alyson Spiro

Graham Walters

Ingrid Wells

Director, David Freeman

Assistant Director, Stephen Langridge

Design, David Roger

Composer, Nigel Osborne

Lighting Design, Peter Mumford

Company Stage Manager, Charmaine Goodchild

Deputy Stage Manager, Mary Madigan

Assistant Stage Manager, Tamar Thomas

Fire Sequence Adviser, Leo Ward

PRELUDE and PROLOGUE

PRELUDE

On the stage

DIRECTOR: Colleagues, and friends, in times of stress,
    have you a notion, can you say
    just what the Theatre needs today,
    or is it anybody's guess?
    All I want for myself's an audience
    equipped with live-and-let-live common sense,
    sitting, relaxed, with wide expectant eyes,
    agog for some theatrical surprise.
    I've kept my finger on the public taste,
    but never have I felt quite so unsure;   10*
    they may not be accustomed to the best,
    but still, they've read, or seen it all before.
    How do we make it all look fresh and new,
    with something for the intellectuals too?
    I want to see those crowds at half-past seven,
    struggling like damned souls to get into Heaven.
    One man can please high, low and middle-brow:
    that is the author: so, friend, help us now.
AUTHOR: Don't speak to me about the many-headed,
    that human plankton, the ticket-buyers!   20
    Their chatter and fidgeting's what one's most dreaded,
    dragging one back from what one most desires.
    The glitter fades like dew, and lets us see
    the gold remaining for Posterity.
ACTOR: Talk of 'Posterity' makes me want to spit!
    Where would we be were I to talk of it?
    Who would amuse the audience in the Present?
    The Future's gain would be the Present's loss.
    An audience of one maybe quite pleasant,
    but actors, who can put a play across,   30
    know that effect and audience both increase
    in direct ratio: so...write a masterpiece,

---

* Line numbers are provided for reference to this translation. They do not
  refer to lines in the original play.

with passion, sensitivity and wit –
and room for us to fool about a bit.
DIRECTOR: And do be sure to make enough things happen.
Action is what they need to set them clapping.
They come to listen and they come to look,
or they could just stay home and read a book.
Variety is all: to be enough
to please a crowd, it must be crowded stuff.   40
And, if the play's consistent, word for word,
they'll still pick out the bits that they preferred.
AUTHOR: But don't you see how dreadful such plays are?
You don't need me: you need a carpenter.
DIRECTOR: Sticks and stones! Unless they're proper fools,
workmen take care to pick the proper tools.
You must remember whom you're writing for:
some come to seek relief from being bored,
some to digest excess of food and booze,
and some, the worst, from reading the reviews.   50
Pack your plays tight, my dear, and when you've packed
          them
with incident and wit enough, we'll act them.
Variety ensures the house is full.
The most the best of us can do's distract them.
To satisfy them is impossible.
You look *distrait*. What is it? Grief or joy?
AUTHOR: Oh, find yourself another office-boy!
The power of speech, the highest human power,
wasted, so you can strut and fret your hour!
The poet moves the heart to joy or anguish,   60
by his essential gift, the power of language.
Who else can call the fragments of Creation
into a whole by pure imagination?
Who sees in storms the tide of human passion?
Who hymns the thought behind the setting sun?
Who plucks the first frail flowers of Spring to fashion
garlands to strew before the Beloved One?
Who makes, from the insignificant green leaves,
wreaths to crown achievement of every kind?

Who can unite the gods, by his beliefs? 70
Man's mighty spirit, in the Poet's mind.
ACTOR: How good it would be if all this fine talk
could be transformed into some good hard work.
Think of a play, as of a love affair:
boy meets girl, loves girl – happens everywhere –
boy loses girl, boy finds girl. As you look,
before you know it, you've a good, fat book.
So do the same, and pick out for the drama,
material from the human panorama;
something which we can all experience, 80
but of which only some can grasp the sense.
Everyone lives, but most of us will die
without discovering The Reason Why:
and anything that can explain our fears
and aspirations runs for years and years.
DIRECTOR: If we might just proceed from words to deeds...
for, to be frank, although your talk is good,
action is what the Theatre really needs –
at least, that's what I've always understood.
Well, then begin! Put Reason into Rhyme. 90
Procrastination is the thief of Time.
You know now what we want – a heady brew
to warm the waiting public through and through.
Our National Theatre, as you are aware,
gives every artist freedom and to spare.
Our Theatre lets each artist try his skill.
This is a special day: take what you will,
don't spare me in the matter of machinery,
have backdrops, trapdoors, all you want of scenery,
Sun, moon, fire, mountains, animals and such; 100
just make sure that it doesn't cost too much.
Now, let Creation's mighty sphere
within this wooden 'O' appear,
and travel, by a transformation scene,
from Heaven to Hell, via all that lies between.

End of Prelude.

PROLOGUE

In Heaven

RAPHAEL: The sun resumes its ancient song,
 with all its brother-spheres competing,
 moving with thunder-claps along,
 its predetermined course completing.
 The sight will cheer the angelic host,
 though what its essence none can see:
 works, high and inconceivable,
 keep their first, glorious mystery.
GABRIEL: And swiftly, baffling thought and sight,
 the splendour of the earth swings round,   10
 exchanging scenes of heavenly light
 for night as dreadful as profound.
 The waves are tossed in wild commotion;
 against the rockface beats the sea;
 and with the planets, rock and ocean
 spin swiftly through Eternity.
MICHAEL: In loud contention, storms are hurled
 from sea to land, from land to sea,
 forming, in fury round the world,
 a chain of mighty agency.   20
 While lightning flames, in wild career,
 light up the thunder on its way,
 Thy messengers, O Lord, revere
 the tranquil motion of Thy day.
ARCHANGELS: Thy sight will cheer the angelic host,
 though what Thy essence none can see.
 Thy works, high, inconceivable,
 keep their first, glorious mystery.
MEPHISTOPHELES: Since you, O Lord, are here, once
         more, to see
 just how the world and we are getting on,   30
 and since you've always been so kind to me,
 here I am, once again, among the throng.
 Forgive me if my diction doesn't fit

34

the lofty tone of all that we just heard;
if I tried eloquence, you'd laugh at it,
if laughter here was not a dirty word.
Planets and stars are not my cup of tea:
the self-inflicted woes of men are all that interest me;
the little god of the world, in the same situation,
as odd as on the first day of Creation.   40
Though life on earth would not be quite
so vile had you not given him that glimpse of heavenly light,
that he calls Reason, but uses, if at all,
to be more animal than any animal.
Lord, with all due respect, he seems to me
one of those long-legged grasshoppers you see
leaping in all directions, flying along,
then lying in the grass, chirping the same old song.
Is he content to lie there? No such luck!
He pokes his nose in every sort of muck.   50
GOD: And is that all you came up here to say?
    Why must you come complaining every day?
    Does nothing ever please you down on earth?
MEPHISTOPHELES: No, Lord, to be quite frank, things
                                    go from bad to worse.
    The torments of Mankind move even me
    to pity, not to plague Humanity.
GOD: You know my servant Faust?
MEPHISTOPHELES: The doctor?
GOD: Yes.
MEPHISTOPHELES: Your servant? One of downright
                                            quirkiness,
    a fool; his habits are not of this world.
    Driven by his obsessions, he is hurled   60
    up into spheres where he himself half knows
    how mad he is, but still the poor man goes
    on hankering after Heaven's brightest star,
    and craving earthly joys of every kind,
    ranging the realm of knowledge near and far,
    finding no harbour for his restless mind.
GOD: He serves me now uncomprehendingly.
    But I shall lead him soon toward the light.

35

The gardener knows, by looking at the tree,
what flowers and fruit lie ripening out of sight.   70
MEPHISTOPHELES: What do you bet you do not lose
    his soul? Provided that you give me leave, of course,
    to lead him down whatever path I choose.
GOD: While he is still on earth, and still alive,
    try whatever springs to mind:
    Men make mistakes, till they learn not to strive.
MEPHISTOPHELES: Thank you for that, Lord: humankind
    I've never much liked after death, to tell the truth.
    I far prefer the full, pink bloom of youth.
    To me, a corpse is *not* a welcome guest: 80
    'Cat-and-mouse' is the game that I play best.
GOD: Try to seduce his soul from its true source.
    'Behold, all that he hath is in thy power;
    only upon himself lay not thy hand' –
    and if things do not go quite as you planned,
    admit, with shame, among those souls you would devour
    are some that can't be moved, even by you,
    from the good they dimly, stubbornly pursue.
MEPHISTOPHELES: Done! But if I win, and he fails the test,
    give me a triumph, trumpets and the rest.   90
    With dust he'll happily his hunger slake,
    Like my notorious relative, the snake.
GOD: There too you are free to do your best.
    I never hated beings of your style:
    of all the spirits of denial,
    I find the joker irritates me least.
    (*Heaven closes: GOD leaves with the ANGELS.*)
MEPHISTOPHELES: (*Alone.*)
    I like to see the Old Man now and then,
    and always take care not to break with Him.
    He's very decent, quite the gentleman,
    letting poor devils like me speak with Him.   100

End of Prologue.

PART ONE

1: Night – Faust's study[*]

A high-vaulted, Gothic room. FAUST discovered, restless, at his desk.

FAUST: Here I am, then. Philosophy
    behind me, Law and Medicine too,
    and – to my cost – Theology...
    all studied, grimly sweated through;
    and here I sit, as big a fool
    as when I first attended school.
    True, I surpass the dull incompetents,
    doctors, pastors and masters, and the rest,
    for whom there is no bliss but ignorance,
    but this pre-eminence I now detest.
    All my laborious studies only show
    that Nothing is the most we ever know.   10
    Scruples I've laid aside, doubts as well;
    I have no fear of the Devil or Hell –
    and this is what robs me of all delight.
    I cannot boast that what I know is right;
    I cannot boast my teaching will ever find
    a way to improve or to convert Mankind.
    Meanwhile I live in poverty;
    no dog would choose to live like me.
    And so the rites of Magic I rehearse,
    to probe the secrets of the Universe;   20
    to learn its mysteries and recognise
    the force that binds all Nature's energies;
    to see Creation's principles at work,
    and waste no more time on the trade of talk.

    O Moon, would you could look your last
    upon my pain, as in the past
    you've watched me, quietly, at my books
    and papers, with sad, friendly looks.
    O, could I, on the mountain's height,
    wander in your kindly light,   30

---

[*] Scene numbers are provided for reference to this translation. They do not
  appear in the original play.

through mountain caves with spirits sail,
cross and recross the twilit vale;
freed from the fumes of science, renew
my spirit in your healing dew.

Imprisoned in my library,
with stacks of papers, ceiling-high,
worm-eaten junk, pell-mell together hurled,
with scientific instruments,
a valueless inheritance. 40
This is my world! Here's what is called a world!

Instead of living in the world
where God created men to be,
you live, hemmed in by smoke and mould,
with skeletons for company.

Away with it, then! Leave it all behind!
A better, secret mentor springs to mind.
From this I know there is a world elsewhere;
what other guide do I need to take me there?
Spirit speaks unto spirit, and divines 50
the meaning of mysterious designs.
Spirits, I feel you, hovering near me;
answer me, now, if you can hear me!
(*Opening the book, he finds the sign of the Macrocosm.*)
Ah! sudden joy leaps through me at this sight,
flooding my being, filling every sense;
a new and holy feeling of delight
runs through each vein, each nerve, glowing, intense.
Was it a God who patterned out this sign,
by which my spirit's inward strife is stilled,
by which my wretched heart with joy is filled, 60
by which, with mystic power, the grand design
of omnipresent Nature is revealed?
Am I a god? Light dawns on me:
in these clear symbols I perceive the whole
of Nature's mighty engine, open to my soul,
and grasp the meaning of the prophecy:
'The spirit world's no occult sphere;

your heart is dead, your sense withdrawn.
Seeker of knowledge, rise, bathe without fear
your human breast in the red of dawn!'   70
(*He gazes at the sign.*)
A great show, but no more than that – a show!
Infinite Nature, where can I grasp you? How?
Where are your breasts, those fountains that maintain
all life throughout the Universe,
at which the parched soul slakes its thirst?
You flow and gush: why do I thirst in vain?
(*He turns the pages of the book impatiently, and comes on the
sign of the Earth-Spirit.*)
How different the effects of this new sign!
Spirit of Earth, we are closer akin;
I feel my powers grow strong within,
as if intoxicated with new wine.   80

I feel the strength to be my fate's defender,
to bear both earthly woe, and earthly splendour,
to grapple with storms, a worthy contender,
and in the grinding shipwreck, not surrender.
The clouds close in above me...
the moon is hidden...
the lamp burns low...
vapours rise...red beams
flicker about my head, and from the roof
a shuddering horror floats down   90
and seizes me.
I feel you, Spirit I have called, you hover near.
It's tearing at my heart. Appear!
At each new pang I feel
my senses reel...
I feel my heart surrender, gripped as if in a vice...
Oh, come! Oh, come, you must, though death should be
                                                          the price!
(*He seizes the book, and pronounces the secret sign of the
Earth-Spirit. A red flame flares up, and in the flame, the
EARTH-SPIRIT appears.*)
EARTH-SPIRIT: Who calls me?
FAUST: Horror!

41

EARTH-SPIRIT: You compel me here.
  You wrestled long to penetrate my sphere,
  and now...   100
FAUST: Oh, God – this sight I cannot bear!
EARTH-SPIRIT: It was I whom your mighty incantation
  invoked: and here I am. What agitation
  seizes you, Faust? Are you the Superman
  who challenged me to come here, who began
  so bravely, but who, as you felt my breath,
  fell down before me, frightened half to death,
  a trembling, writhing, timorous worm?
FAUST: Am I to yield to you, you thing of flame?
  Faust is your equal, Spirit: fear my name!
EARTH-SPIRIT: In the torrents of life, in action's storm,   110
  I weave and wave
  in endless motion
  cradle and grave
  a timeless ocean
  ceaselessly weaving
  the tissue of living
  constantly changing
  blending, arranging
  the humming loom of Time I ply
  and weave the web of Divinity.   120
FAUST: Restless spirit! Ranging from end to end
  of the turning world, how close I feel to Thee!
EARTH-SPIRIT: You're kin to the spirit that you comprehend:
  not me.
  (*The EARTH-SPIRIT vanishes.*)
FAUST: (*Shaken.*)
  Not you?
  Then who?
  Made in the image of God,
  and am I not to be ranked with you?
  (*A knock.*)
  Damnation! Who is it?
WAGNER: Wagner.
FAUST: My student.

42

(*WAGNER enters in nightgown and nightcap, carrying a*   130
lamp. FAUST turns to him impatiently.)

WAGNER: Forgive me, Sir, if I am being imprudent,
    but might I ask if that was Greek that I
    heard you declaiming? From some tragedy?
    I'd like to profit from reciting plays:
    it's taken very seriously nowadays.
    It's often said the theatre's a good teacher,
    and that the actor can instruct the preacher.

FAUST: Yes; when the preacher also is an actor,
    as often is his Lowest Common Factor.
    The only trouble with your preaching actors
    is, they so often preach what they don't practice.   140

WAGNER: But, living in self-inflicted isolation,
    seeing the world as if through a telescope,
    or only on a holiday, can we hope
    to influence, or rule men by persuasion?
    The speaker's style alone can win the heart,
    and I am less than expert in that art.

FAUST: Good sense and single-mindedness,
    above all else, ensure a man's success.

WAGNER: Dear God, how short is Life, how long is Art!
    We climb a hard road to the fountainhead,   150
    and by the time we've learned the smallest part
    of what we want, as like as not, we're dead.
    I read a deal of History, to transport
    myself into the Spirit of the Past,
    to find out what great men have said and thought,
    and see the glorious heights we've reached at last.

FAUST: 'The Spirit of the Past'? An old-clothes closet,
    a rubbish heap where 'great men' can deposit
    the trash they make of their own generations.

WAGNER: But surely, Sir, Mankind's imagination's   160
    what we want to understand – his mind?

FAUST: To understand? And how is that defined?
    Some did not veil their thoughts from men, but tried
    to show their hearts – and they were crucified.
    But now, my friend, it's time we were adjourning.

WAGNER: I could have stayed for hours to hear such
learning.

> I hope I haven't kept you up all night,
> though cultured conversation's a delight.
> But since tomorrow will be Easter Day,
> I'll put some further questions, if I may.　　170
> I've learnt much by devoted studying
> but cannot rest till I know everything.
> (*He goes out.*)

FAUST: The only ones who never give up hope

> are those whose minds are fixed on trivial things:
> they dig for treasure, but are glad to grope
> for earthworms to reward their blunderings.
> And yet, for once, he has my gratitude.
> Despair and madness were about to blast
> the power of sense – the vision was too vast.
> I shrank, a dwarf, before that monstrous attitude.　　180
> For, though I could compel it to appear,
> I had no power to detain it here.
> But in that moment, drenched with ecstasy,
> I felt my pigmy self grow great;
> it thrust me down, and cruelly sentenced me
> once more to Man's uncertain fate.

> Am I God's image? Shall I rank with gods?
> No – I am only kin to worms, and clods
> of common clay, the pounded dust which packs
> the shelves that wall in academic hacks.　　190
> Is it here I'll discover what I lack?
> Read through a thousand books, and all to find
> Humanity puts itself upon the rack,
> and Happiness is rare among Mankind?
> What are you grinning at, you hollow skull?
> Because your brain, like mine, once sought the spark
> of Truth, but fell a victim to mere dull
> confusion, and was swallowed in the dark?
> My complex instruments stand mocking me:
> to Nature's secrets they were to be the key.　　200
> But if she will not teach her mystery,

there's little merit in Technology.
My father's junk, unused, inherited –
what we can't use does nothing but impede.
Nothing is owned unearned, unmerited:
necessity creates the only things we need.

What thing is that, though, which impels my gaze?
Why is that phial a magnet to my sight?
A radiance plays around me, like the rays
of moonlight, in the forest, in the night.   210

In you I honour human art and skill,
quintessence of all soothing anodynes,
which every rare and deadly power combines,
now, for your master, all your strength distil!

Another day! A chariot of fire
comes near. New roads lie open to me. I
shall pierce the veil that hides what we desire,
break through to realms of abstract energy.
But, earthbound still, a worm, how may I earn
this higher life, this heavenly rebirth?   220
Only if I can resolutely turn
my back on the sun that kindles life on earth:
summon my daring to pass through the gate
which most men shun in every way they can.
Now I must show, in action, that a man
may be as free as gods, and be as great;
not shudder at the dreadful pit, that harrows
our fancy, self-condemned to its own dark fear,
but struggle to force a passage through the narrow
straits, at whose mouth the flames of Hell appear;   230
and take this step with calm determination,
though it should bring with it annihilation.

This draught intoxicates as it is drawn.
The dark narcotic flood streams out to fill
the cup: juice I have chosen and distilled
to be my last drink, drunk with firm soul and will,
in solemn salutation to the coming dawn!
(*He raises the cup to his lips. Clangour of bells, and chanting.*)

Music of God, so powerful and so sweet,
why do you seek me out here in the dust?
Go entertain the faithful, if you must,   240
I hear the message, but my faith is weak.
A miracle is religion's dearest child:
the Easter hymn brings childhood flooding back to me.
I must retrace my steps, be reconciled
to all that made my last step a possibility.
Ring, sing of resurrection and rebirth!
My eyes are wet: I have returned to earth.

2: Outside the city gate

People of all sorts out walking.

STUDENT: God, but those girls can get a head of steam on!
    Come on, we'll find 'em later, never fear.
    I need a drink – I'm thirsty as a demon,
    I'd sell my soul for a pipe and a glass of beer.
GIRL: You see that boy, the fair one in the hat?
    Just look at him. I think it's a disgrace
    they should be running after girls like that;
    pretty, I dare say, but so commonplace.
CITIZEN: Sir, the new government is no damn good,
    and daily getting worse: I said it would.   10
    What is it doing for the country, eh?
    Standards of living are falling day by day:
    meanwhile inflation soars. No, Sir, the fact is
    nothing is certain, except death and taxes.
ANOTHER CITIZEN: My dear, today's a holiday weekend:
    I want to read of nothing else but wars
    happening to someone else, my friend,
    somewhere like Turkey, far from our shores.
    Stand at the window, drinking half the night,
    thinking 'How lovely not to have to fight.'   20
THIRD CITIZEN: My dear good chap, I really am inclined to
    agree. Let them break heads if they've a mind to.
    If I can keep what I'm accustomed to,
    I really don't much care what they may do.

OLD WOMAN: (*To the GIRLS.*)
    Well, look at you now, dressed to beat the band!
    To look at you's to love you, so it is.
    Oh, hoity-toity! Tell me what it is
    you want, and I might lend a helping hand.
GIRL: Don't be seen talking to that sour old bitch;
    you never know, they tell me she's a witch.   30
SECOND GIRL: I know: she said before I was much older,
    I'd meet a boy, a big strong handsome soldier,
    She said she'd seen it in the crystal ball,
    but if she did, I can't find him at all.
SOLDIERS: Castles display
    towers and turrets,
    girls display proud
    and contrary spirits.
    Both are our prey!
    Bold the adventure,   40
    but handsome the pay.

    Trumpets and drums
    call us away,
    to laughter or death,
    still we obey.
    Life is a battlefield,
    mis'ry and splendour,
    castles and girls,
    both must surrender.
    Bold the adventure,   50
    but handsome the pay;
    tomorrow the soldiers
    march off and away.
FAUST: Here in the cheerful, noisy crowd, I can
    at last be what I always was – a man.
WAGNER: To walk with you, Sir, is for me
    a real experience for the mind:
    not that I'd come here on my own. You see,
    I hate vulgarity of any kind.
    That screaming, fiddling, brawling, I detest.   60
    That is no way to occupy one's leisure.

Dancing and shouting, they're like things possessed.
How can they call that music, let alone pleasure?
OLD MAN: Doctor, good day! How good to see
    you join us in our Easter celebrations.
    A lot of people here can be
    grateful to you and your father's ministrations.
    During the epidemic, you and he
    came to our houses, tended us, and cared
    for us without thought for yourselves. You never spared   70
    yourselves, so you yourselves were spared.
WAGNER: I imagine it must make you very proud
    to hear such tributes from a grateful crowd.
FAUST: A few steps more, to that stone over there,
    and we can rest. I've often sat and thought
    alone here, torturing myself with prayer
    and fasting, firm in my beliefs, and sought,
    and hoped to find, in tears, upon my knees,
    a way to end that terrible disease,
    to force God's hand, compel him to a peace.   80
    The crowd's applause, for father as for son,
    now sounds to me like blame. If you could see
    inside my heart, you'd know at once that we
    deserve no part of all the fame we won.
    My father's honourable pursuit of Science
    led him into dark by-ways, dubious paths, where he,
    seeking to plumb the central mystery,
    made his own rules, set others at defiance.
    With adepts and initiates, he would be
    locked in his dark alchemic shrine,   90
    with endless recipes and formulae,
    forcing disparate elements to combine.
    In tepid baths, the ardent, red-gold Lion was wed
    to the white-silver Lily: from one bed
    of glass into another, he teased the bridal pair,
    subjecting them to fiercer heat, till there,
    in the retort, was seen the perfect presence
    of the Young Queen, in rainbow iridescence.
    That was the medicine – but the patients died.
    The question 'Who survived?' was set aside.   100

We were a worse plague than the epidemic.
I poisoned thousands: how could I have dreamed
I'd live to hear their murderers esteemed?
WAGNER: Oh, surely, Sir, the question's academic.
FAUST: Happy the man who can still hope to swim
    clear of the sea of Error's choking weeds!
    What Man does *not* know, is just what he needs,
    while what he *does* know, is no use to him.
    The sun is setting here, and moving on
    to waken life elsewhere. Our day is gone.   110
    Oh, God, for wings to follow, unafraid,
    into a sunset that would never fade!
    To see, in everlasting evening light,
    the silent world below me; sunset's beams
    calming each valley, gilding every height,
    as silver rivers meet in golden streams.
    Nor could the progress of my god-like ride
    by savage mountain chasms be denied.
    But look! the sea, with quiet sun-warmed bays,
    reveals itself to my astonished gaze: 120
    Heaven above me, and below, the sea.
    Meanwhile the sun sets on this dream of radiant things.
    An earthly body cannot easily
    fly on the spirit's upward-soaring wings.
    Yet instinct, born in all of us, bids us rise
    and struggle upwards, till we touch the skies.
WAGNER: I've days myself when such things spring to mind:
    though never anything of quite that kind.
    I never envied birds their wings: and such
    things as woods and fields don't interest me much.   130
    I prefer reading, pleasures of the study
    to all the so-called pleasures of the body.
    There is more taste of Heaven in a book,
    than in all Nature, wherever we may look.
FAUST: Friend, you are lucky to have *one* obsession:
    take care you do not cultivate another.
    Two souls within me wrestle for possession,
    and neither will surrender to his brother.
    One is of the senses, sensual,

slaking his appetites like an animal: 140
the other strives for purity of mind,
to leave the world and all its works behind.
Oh, if there are spirits listening in the air,
descend now from your golden stratosphere;
carry me off to new life – anywhere!
If I possessed a magic cloak, to bear
me bodily away to distant lands,
I'd not exchange it for the finest wear
of a king: no one should take it from my hands.

WAGNER: Hush, Doctor! though it may be superstition, 150
I do not like this jesting with religion.
Do not call up the powers that lie in wait,
to practise mischief on Man's poor estate.
They hover threatening in the air,
and perils for Mankind prepare.
Let us go in; the world is turning grey,
the air is chilly, mist succeeds the day.
It's good at night to get back to one's room.
What's wrong? Is something out there in the gloom?

FAUST: D'you see that dog?

WAGNER: Why, yes, Sir, now you mention. 160
I noticed it just now, but paid it no attention.

FAUST: Then pay some now. What sort of dog is it?

WAGNER: *Canis domesticus*, a poodle, black,
snuffling round to find his master's track.

FAUST: Look how he keeps on circling, round and round,
closer to us: d'you notice how the ground
flames as he runs, or do my eyes deceive me?

WAGNER: An optical illusion, Sir, believe me.

FAUST: The circle's narrowing, he's coming near.

WAGNER: It's just a poodle, Sir, no spirits here. 170

FAUST: Of course, you must be right. I see no trace
of anything out of the commonplace.
Come on, then! Look! He's coming, do you see?

WAGNER: Normal canine behaviour, seems to me.
A dog, well-trained, obedient and active,
is something even wise men find attractive.
(*They enter the gate of the city.*)

3: Faust's study

FAUST: (*Entering followed by the poodle.*)
Fields and meadows are left behind:
over them night's veil lies spread.
And now the pure, untrammelled mind
awakens, filled with holy dread.
Now our savage urges sleep,
lawless passions droop and nod:
in our hearts lie, fixed and deep,
love of Man and love of God.

Down, poodle, down! Stop sniffing at the door.
Go to your cushion! Don't growl any more!   10

Back inside our narrow cell,
here, where the lamp serenely glows,
within the heart that truly knows
itself, we can feel all is well.
Once more the voice of Reason speaks;
Hope blooms with her accustomed force.
Man longs to tap life's springs, and seeks
the fountainhead, Life's primal source.

Poodle, be quiet! that ugly growl
jars on the elevated feelings in my soul.   20
There may be men who mock the good,
growl at the beautiful, the true,
and all they haven't understood:
does that mean dogs must do so too?

My good intentions ebb: already I
feel my contentment, like a spring, run dry –
a human failing, with this compensation,
it sets us hankering after revelation.
And where in purer form can such things be
than in the Testament of Christianity?   30
St John: 'In the Beginning was the Word.'
Can words be as powerful as is here inferred?
Words are by Intelligence designed;
it must mean – in the Beginning was the Mind.

No! Mind or Thought alone are not the source
of Life. In the Beginning was the Force.
But even as I say it, I'm aware
it's not enough to leave the matter there.
At last! The spirit gives me the exact
translation: In the Beginning was the Act!   40

Poodle, if I'm to share this room with you,
just leave off whining for an hour or two.
Howling and growling –
if you're causing all this bother,
then one of us or the other
will have to go.
So!

I don't wish to appear a churlish host,
but this room's big enough for one, at most.
Poodle! The door! Oh, God, what's happening?   50
Behind the stove some dreadful thing
takes shape. The dog! The dog! Growing to monstrous size,
with slavering red fangs and burning eyes,
the mighty daemon now I recognise.
To kennel up the hounds of Hell,
rehearse the quadripartite spell:
Clavis Salomonis, serve me well!

Salamander, take fire!
Turn, Undine, in the wave!
Sylphide, vanish in air!   60
Gnome, drudge and slave!

Vanish in flames,
Salamander!
Mingle in streams,
Undine!
Blaze in the beauty of stars,
Sylphide!
Minister to our need,
Incubus! Incubus!
Come forth from him, Diabolus!   70

Nothing.

None of the elemental four
lurks in the beast.
He lies quiet now, grinning as before,
not put out in the least.

If, thing of evil,
you be a devil,
look on this sign, the Name revere
of Him, transpierced with nail and spear!

Behind the stove, held by my spell,   80
his hair stands up, he starts again to swell,
and now, unable to resist
my art, he threatens to dissolve in mist.
Come down! This is no idle threat:
with holy fire I'll dowse you yet.
Do not await the triple glowing light,
the Trinity of Might,
the burning flames
embodied in the sacred triple names.
Wait not upon my magic's highest power!   90
(*As the mist sinks, MEPHISTOPHELES appears from
behind the stove, dressed as a travelling scholar.*)
MEPHISTOPHELES: A lot of noise. What might the
                                    gentleman require?
FAUST: Was that the poodle's inmost core? That all?
     A wandering scholar! Now, I have to smile.
MEPHISTOPHELES: Allow me to salute you, in fine style.
     I got into a pretty sweat to come at all.
FAUST: What is your name?
MEPHISTOPHELES: The question seems absurd
     from someone who so denigrates the Word,
     who, unaffected by mere outward show,
     finds, in Creation's depths, what he wants to know.
FAUST: With gentlemen like you one must be able   100
     to sum you up by some descriptive label,
     like Prince of Darkness, Tempter, Lord of Flies,
     Old Gentleman, Adversary, Father of Lies.
     Who are you then?

MEPHISTOPHELES: Part of the power which would
   work only Evil, but produces Good.
FAUST: Conundrums now. What do you mean?
MEPHISTOPHELES: That I
   am the spirit that must constantly deny.
   And quite right too: all things that live and grow
   deserve to have a final overthrow.
   (Better if they did not begin.)   110
   So, everything that you call Sin,
   Death and Destruction – all that's meant
   by 'Evil' – is my element.
FAUST: 'Part of the power', you called yourself just now.
   You seem complete enough to me. So, how?
MEPHISTOPHELES: I spoke the simple truth. Man is a fool
   if he believes the world's a perfect whole.
   I am part of a part that, at the start, was All;
   part of the darkness that, though once complete,
   gave birth to light, which fights now to defeat   120
   its mother, darkness, but is doomed to fall,
   because it's fettered to material forms.
   Light streams from Matter; Matter it adorns,
   but Matter hinders Light from getting free.
   I trust it won't be long before I see
   Light sharing Matter's final destiny.
FAUST: I think I understand your situation.
   Failing to bring about annihilation
   on the grand scale, you start with something small?
MEPHISTOPHELES: And frankly, we're not doing well at all. 130
   The Nothing, of which I am part, has found
   some crude force in the world which can confound
   our fiercest efforts. Tempest, fire and flood,
   natural disasters…all no good.
   The earth endures, and so does Life, what's worse;
   plants, men and animals fill the universe.
   The more I slay, the more they replicate;
   enough to make one want to emigrate.
   From elements of water, air and earth,
   Life teems in sensual, unthinking birth.   140

Fire is still mine, but Fire and Fire alone,
or I'd not have a thing to call my own.
FAUST: The healthy, active instinct of creation
    will everlastingly resist
    the power of malicious condemnation
    bunched in your sterile, passive fist.
    Curious child of Chaos, why don't you
    find some more profitable thing to do?
MEPHISTOPHELES: As matter for a conversation
    that well deserves consideration.   150
    But, would you mind now, if I took my leave?
FAUST: Why you should ask, I really can't conceive.
    Now that we have learned to know
    each other, you are free to come and go.
MEPHISTOPHELES: Not quite: there is a slight impediment
    to my departure; I must own I am
    somewhat incommoded by your pentagram.
FAUST: The star? You find that inconvenient?
    But if this stops you, child of Hell and Sin,
    from getting out, then how did you get in?   160
MEPHISTOPHELES: If you look carefully, you'll see that it
    is not drawn quite correctly; there's a bit
    left open here, at one of the outer angles.
FAUST: There now! How Chance the slyest soul entangles!
    You are my prisoner, then? I never meant
    to do this. It was the purest accident.
MEPHISTOPHELES: The poodle didn't think, he just
                                    bounced in.
    But things have now assumed another shape;
    the Devil's in the house and can't escape.
FAUST: What is the matter with the window, then?   170
MEPHISTOPHELES: A law that ghosts and devils must obey:
    whichever way they entered, that's the way
    they go out by. The entrance they are free
    to choose, but not the exit.
FAUST: I am glad to see
    Hell has its rules and regulations too.
    In which case, a contract made with you
    would be adhered to?

MEPHISTOPHELES: To the very letter.
     But these things all take time. It might be better
     if we could talk of all this later. Now
     I really need your gracious leave to go.   180
FAUST: I never asked you to come here. You fell
     into a trap that was not of my making.
     Let him who holds the Devil, hold him well:
     another time he's not so easily taken.
MEPHISTOPHELES: Well, if you will, your wish is my
                                  command,
     but on this one condition, understand:
     that if I am to occupy your leisure,
     you'll let me use my arts to give you pleasure.
FAUST: Feel free: the mere fact that you are remaining
     to do all this, I find quite entertaining.   190
MEPHISTOPHELES: Your senses, friend, will find, in this
                                  one hour
     fulfilment and enjoyment of more power
     than you will know in one whole year!
     And what the delicate spirits sing,
     the ravishing images they bring,
     are no mere charms to lull the ear.
     They will beguile your sense of smell,
     quicken your sense of taste as well,
     and feeling too, you need not fear.
     Preparation we do not need.   200
     We are all met. We can proceed!
SPIRITS CHORUS: Vanish, you sombre
     ceilings above us
     scudding and fleeting
     the dark cloud no longer
     threatening hovers
     starlight is shimmering
     suns of a glimmering
     radiance greeting
     the children of light   210
     who throng in the air
     infinite longings
     follow them there

their beauty covers
the gardens where lovers
deep in their visions
lost in emotion
swear their devotion
for life to each other
wine gushes streaming   220
foaming and creaming
through gemstones in fountains
leaving the mountains
for lakes brightly gleaming
birds fly South to lightness
the islands of brightness
that ride on the ocean
for ever in motion
where joyfully round us
choruses sound as   230
we see them advancing
swaying and dancing
some of them climbing
over the hills
some of them swimming
where the sea swells
some hovering in space
yet all of them are
seeking the far
life-loving star   240
and its infinite grace.

MEPHISTOPHELES: Well done, my dainty boys, he is

asleep!

Your song has sunk him into slumber deep.
This concert puts me firmly in your debt.
But now to break this tiresome spell,
and cross the threshold, back to Hell,
I need the teeth of a good, strong rat;
no difficulty finding that.

The lord of rats, and lord of mice,
lord of frogs, bugs, flies and lice,   250

commands you, servant rat, appear,
come out and gnaw the threshold there!
Quick, get to work! The angle that I can't
get past is on that side, out at the front.
Just one more bite! That's it. I can't complain.
Now, sweet dreams, Faust, until we meet again!

FAUST: (*Waking up.*)

Cheated again! Was the Devil here?
How did the spirits disappear?
Was it a dream? Was it a riddle?
Was it a poodle? Or was it Evil?   260
Here I am at the middle of the way,
too young to be without desires, too old
to be content to throw my time away.
What comfort can the mortal world still hold?
'Renunciation: learn to do without!',
they all say: they don't know what it's about.
I wake each morning with a start of pain,
knowing that by the time each day is done,
I shall be forced to acknowledge, once again,
not one desire has been fulfilled – not one.   270
And, once again, as Night descends,
and I lie staring on my bed,
the Hell that is inside me sends
terrible dreams to fill my head.
Deep in my soul, God stirs the springs,
but cannot move external things.
Existence is become a mere, dead weight:
Would death could free me from the life I hate!

MEPHISTOPHELES: Knock knock.

FAUST: Come in.

MEPHISTOPHELES: Knock knock.

FAUST: Who's there?

MEPHISTOPHELES: It's me.

FAUST: I said 'Come in.'

MEPHISTOPHELES: Knock knock.

FAUST: What is it, man?   280

MEPHISTOPHELES: You have to say 'Come in' three
                              times before I can.

FAUST: Can what?

MEPHISTOPHELES: Come in, of course.

FAUST: Come in then.

MEPHISTOPHELES: Thanks. I can see
   you don't look well. What's wrong? How do
   you like the new clothes I put on for you?
   You could do worse than follow my example.
   Life is just full of pleasures you should sample.
   Changing one's clothes is the easiest way to give
   an added impulse to the Will to Live.

FAUST: I fear the very bravest of attire
   would be unlikely to revive my fire.   290
   I drag my life round like an endless train.

MEPHISTOPHELES: Life may be loss, but is Death such
                                 a gain?

FAUST: If it should come in a victorious hour,
   or in a lover's arms... The spirit's power
   I felt last night – how long ago? – why could not he
   have drawn me up in mist into Eternity?

MEPHISTOPHELES: Later that night, though, was a
                     chance not wasted,
   when someone let the poison go untasted?

FAUST: Do you spend much of your free time in spying?

MEPHISTOPHELES: I'm not omniscient yet – but I keep
                          trying. 300
   This playing at self-pity's useless, since
   it's like a vulture, feeding on your mind.
   The worst of company can still convince
   you that you're still a man, part of Mankind.
   I do not mean, in any way, by that to set
   you with the Great Unwashed; I may not be
   the most distinguished man you've ever met,
   but still, if you would care to come with me,
   we could make common cause. – Here's my proposal:
   I place myself at your disposal,   310
   however it's expedient.
   I am your squire, your slave, your most obedient.

FAUST: And how do I repay these services?

MEPHISTOPHELES: Plenty of time to think about that.
FAUST: No!
    The Devil is an egoist. I know
    how you deal with Mankind: the emphasis
    is not on charity; so say what your
    conditions are, just so that I may see
    how dangerous such service is to me.
MEPHISTOPHELES: I undertake to be your servant here,   320
    and execute your wishes tirelessly:
    and when we meet together 'over there',
    then you can do the very same for me.
FAUST: That 'over there' has never mattered
    to me. Let this world first be shattered.
    New worlds can fill the void. For good or ill,
    this earth will yield such pleasures as are mine
    and on my sorrows too *this* sun can shine,
    and come the day I'm ready to resign
    all this, the rest does not concern me, come what will.   330
MEPHISTOPHELES: Now that's the proper spirit! Let us
                                   make
    a contract. Then I'll undertake
    to show what I can do, and give you more
    than any man has ever had before.
FAUST: Poor devil, have you anything to give?
    Did any mighty spirit ever live
    that you could fathom, in all your length of days?
    Yours is the bread that cannot satisfy;
    your gold runs through the hand like mercury;
    yours is the game that no one wins who plays.   340
    The girl you'd give me would, while she was mine,
    eye up the man next door, and the divine
    joy of ambition falls like a shooting star.
    Where are the fruits that rot before they're picked? Where are
    the trees that put forth new green every day?
    The day your flattering lies persuade me
    to think well of myself – the day that I
    become a slave to pleasures that degrade me,
    that day's my last – I'll be content to die.
    Is it a wager?

MEPHISTOPHELES: Done!
FAUST: Done!
MEPHISTOPHELES: Done!
FAUST: And done!   350
   If ever, as Time flows by us, I should say:
   'This moment is so beautiful − let it stay!',
   that is the moment when you will have won.
   For me, the passing bell can sound,
   and from my service you'll be free:
   for me, the clock will cease its round,
   and Time exist no more for me.
MEPHISTOPHELES: Remember what you've said. I shan't
                            forget.
FAUST: That is a thing to which you've every right.
   I make no frivolous, presumptuous claim.   360
   I am a slave, while in my present state;
   yours, or whoever's − what's there in a name?
MEPHISTOPHELES: Since accidents can happen, one
                         thing more...
   could you oblige me with a signature?
FAUST: In black and white? You pedant! How absurd!
   If you knew men, you'd know that they can keep their word.
   Well, well, poor devil, how is it to be?
   On parchment, marble, brass, or what you will −
   engrave it, carve it, sign it with a quill?
   The choice is yours − it's all the same to me.   370
MEPHISTOPHELES: No earthly need to get on your high
                         horse.
   This paper here will do quite well, of course.
   And sign it with a little drop of blood.
FAUST: If you think it will do you any good,
   I'll share your melodramatic mummery.
MEPHISTOPHELES: Blood has a very special quality.
FAUST: You need not fear contractual breach from me.
   What I have promised here is nothing more
   than all my energy has striven for.
   I reached too high, and now I see,   380
   you are the fittest company for me.

The great Earth-Spirit threw me down, denied
me; Nature slammed her door, left me outside.
My chain of thought is broken, and my mind
despises learning now, of every kind.
Let us plunge into Passion's hectic dance,
balanced upon the rolling wave of Chance,
where pain is mixed with pleasure, failure with success:
no man can be in action *and* at rest.

MEPHISTOPHELES: No bounds are set to what you may
enjoy. 390

FAUST: Didn't you hear? I do not ask for joy:
excitement, yes, the agony of elation,
hatred in love, the mania of depression.
No more the slave of books, I take my place
among Mankind at last, to share their common destiny,
and when my mind encompasses Humanity,
I'll share the shipwreck of the human race.

MEPHISTOPHELES: Take an old hand's advice: millennia
I have been chewing on this bitter cud.
And no man, from the cradle to the bier, 400
can keep down that eternal, barren food.
The Universe was made for God alone.
He suns himself in everlasting light,
us He casts into darkness on our own,
while you live in alternate day and night.

FAUST: What am I then, if God should bar
all my achievement, my ability,
make my ambition impossibility?

MEPHISTOPHELES: You are, when it comes down to it…
what you are.
Dress up in wigs as lavish as you choose, 410
put on twenty-four-inch platform shoes,
you still remain, forever – what you are.

FAUST: I feel as if I'd drummed into my brain
the wealth of human knowledge all in vain.
I finally stand back, only to find
no new-born power rising in my mind.
Not one hair's breadth is added to my height,
nor am I nearer to the Infinite.

MEPHISTOPHELES: You look at things like deaf and
                                   dumb men do.
  Be wise, or life will run away from you. 420
  Good grief! You have your hands and feet;
  your head, your eyes, your three-piece suite.
  So use them! Sometimes indiscretions
  are our most valuable possessions.
  If I grasp pleasures I have thirsted for,
  are they less mine for that? No! They are more.
  I tell you this: your barren intellectual
  is like a cow, on hard and stony ground,
  which evil spirits lead in ineffectual
  circles, while fields of grass lie all around. 430
  You think too much. Just let it be,
  and come out in the world with me.
FAUST: How to begin?
MEPHISTOPHELES: Just leave. Now. Just hold steady –
  and we can go as soon as you've made ready.
  (*FAUST leaves.*)
  Reason and knowledge – all that stands
  between Mankind and Satan's hands –
  once reject them...he will be
  mine – and unconditionally.
  Since Destiny has given him a soul
  that can't be happy with a passive role, 440
  I now propose to lead him in a dance
  of quite breath-taking insignificance,
  till he sticks fast, immobilised by greed,
  in full realisation of his deed.
  Whether or not he bargains with the Devil
  he's done for either way...
FAUST: (*Re-entering.*)   What means of travel
  had you in mind? Where are the horses? Where
  is the coach, the grooms?
MEPHISTOPHELES: Our equipage is here.
  We merely have to spread this cloak out wide,
  and we're assured of a safe and pleasant ride. 450
  Only, please, on this great step for Mankind,

we'll leave the heavy suitcases behind.
A little inflammable gas, which I'll ignite,
will lift us quickly, if we travel light.
Just shut your eyes, and it will soon be over.
Congratulations on *La Vita Nuova*!

4: Auerbach's cellar in Leipzig

A drinking party.

BRANDER: 'In a cellar lived a rat,
    that fed on lard and butter,
    and grew a paunch as round and fat
    as that of Martin Luther.
    But then the cook spread arsenic
    which made him feel as weak and sick
    as if he was in love again.'
CHORUS: 'As if he was in love again!'
BRANDER: 'In broad daylight and agony,
    he ran into the kitchen,   10
    fell by the hearth and piteously
    lay panting there and twitching.
    The poisoner laughed: "Now there's a joke;
    the poor old thing's about to croak,
    as if he was in love again." '
CHORUS: 'As if he was in love again!'
FROSCH: Does no one want a drink, a laugh?
    Sitting round with funeral faces…
    What is the matter? You're not half
    as bright as a bunch of mental cases.   20
BRANDER: Whose fault is that? You usually give the lead
    if silliness and smut is what we need.
FROSCH: (*Pouring a glass over his head.*)
    Well, there's a start!
BRANDER: You filthy little beast!
FROSCH: I gave you what you asked me for, at least!
SIEBEL: Anyone quarrels, chuck him out!
    Let's have a song, now, good and loud!
    Tralala!

ALTMEYER: Dear God, be quiet! Do you call that singing?
    Bring me some cotton-wool. My ears are ringing.
SIEBEL: It's when the room reverberates that we
    appreciate a basso's quality.   30
FROSCH: If he objects, then chuck him out.
    Laaa!
ALTMEYER: Laaa!
TUTTI: Laaa!
FROSCH: Right! All got the note?
    (*Sings.*)
    'The Holy Roman Empire, now,
    what keeps it all together?'
BRANDER: A rotten song! Political to boot!
    A wretched song! You should thank God, in prayer,
    the Roman Empire isn't your affair.
    I see it personally as clear profit
    that I'm not Chancellor or Emperor of it.
    Still, we all need a leader, I should hope: 40
    so I suggest that we elect a Pope.
    You know the qualities we need
    to help a man like that succeed.
FROSCH: (*Singing.*)
    'O, sweetest Philomel above,
    Bear thousand greetings to my love...'
    (*FAUST enters with MEPHISTOPHELES.*)
MEPHISTOPHELES: I thought I ought to bring you first
                            to see
    a little jovial society.
    Observe how smoothly Life can just slip by.
    These people make each day a holiday.
    With little wit, but zest in generous measure,   50
    they each pursue their little round of pleasure,
    like kittens running after their own tails.
    As long as they don't complain of being hung over,
    and their credit with the landlord never fails,
    they live without a care, like pigs in clover.
BRANDER: Travellers, at a glance: how easily one may
    see they are foreigners in every way.
    Haven't been here an hour yet, I'd say.

FROSCH: Right! Leipzig's a town where people come to stay
    to get some tone, like Paris, only more.   60
SIEBEL: What sort of fellows do you take them for?
FROSCH: Important people, incognito. Those
  dissatisfied expressions aren't a pose.
BRANDER: Tcha! Actors at the best, I bet.
ALTMEYER: May be.
FROSCH: You wait, I'll get it from them yet.
MEPHISTOPHELES: These people simply fail to recognise
  the Devil, standing before their very eyes.
FAUST: Good evening, gentlemen!
SIEBEL: Gentlemen, the same
  to you!
    (*With a glance at MEPHISTOPHELES.*)
           (That one would seem to be a little lame.)
MEPHISTOPHELES: Just now, correct me if I'm wrong,   70
  did we hear voices raised in song?
FROSCH: Are you an amateur? D'you have some skill?
MEPHISTOPHELES: My lack of it's made up for in good
                            will.
ALTMEYER: Give us a song.
MEPHISTOPHELES: A dozen.
SIEBEL: But a new refrain!
MEPHISTOPHELES: A little thing we just brought back
                      from Spain.

  (*Sings.*)
  'A king once had a flea, Sirs,
  a large and lordly one:
  he loved it well, did he, Sirs,
  he loved it like a son.
  His tailor he did summon: 80
  "The young scamp must have clothes!
  And nothing mean or common,
  but doublet, cloak and hose!"

  'In silk the flea was dressed, now,
  in velvet rich arrayed;
  he'd ribbons on his breast, now,
  and orders there displayed.

The king gave him a dozen
high offices of state;
and quite soon all his cousins   90
were courtiers as great.

'Then from the royal throne-room,
down to the servants' hall,
the fleas made it their own room,
biting one and all.
And none dared kill the creatures
nor even dared to scratch,
but we give the quietus
to every flea we catch!'
TUTTI: 'But we give the quietus   100
to every flea we catch!'
FROSCH: Bravo! That's the song for me!
SIEBEL: *Sic pereat semper* every pestilent flea!
BRANDER: Bring in the wine! A toast! To Liberty!
MEPHISTOPHELES: A toast to which I'd gladly raise a glass,
    if the wine here was just a touch more drinkable.
SIEBEL: What's that, Sir? Don't care for our wine?
                                         Unthinkable!
MEPHISTOPHELES: But let us offer you a glass of ours.
    Only I should not like our host upset.
SIEBEL: No fear: I'll take responsibility for that.   110
MEPHISTOPHELES: Give me a gimlet, then.
BRANDER: Whatever for?
    Have you got barrels stacked outside the door?
ALTMEYER: The landlord has some tools there in that basket.
MEPHISTOPHELES: (*Takes the gimlet. To FROSCH.*)
    Now, Sir, what would you like? You need but ask. It's
    yours.
FROSCH: What's that? You have varieties?
MEPHISTOPHELES: Indeed we have. As many as you
                                 please.
ALTMEYER: That's got you interested.
FROSCH: If there's a choice,
                              then mine
    would be for Rheinland, Germany's noblest wine.

MEPHISTOPHELES: (*Boring a hole in the edge of the table, where FROSCH is sitting.*)
Fetch me a bit of wax to make the stoppers. Quick!
ALTMEYER: Pfui, this is nothing but a conjuring trick!   120
MEPHISTOPHELES: (*To BRANDER.*)
What about you, then?
BRANDER: Champagne, my dear Sir:
a foaming, sparkling wine's what I prefer.
(*MEPHISTOPHELES bores holes, one of the others meanwhile having made wax stoppers and plugged the holes with them.*)
One cannot everlastingly decline
foreign imports, banning good things at random.
The French? As a true German I can't stand 'em;
but still, one must admit, they can make wine.
SIEBEL: (*As MEPHISTOPHELES approaches his place.*)
I much prefer a sweet wine to a dry.
MEPHISTOPHELES: What would you say, then, to a fine
                                        Tokay?
ALTMEYER: No, gentlemen, be frank, and look at me;
you're making fun of us, it's plain to see.   130
MEPHISTOPHELES: Tsk! Tsk! with such distinguished
                                        guests,
that would be going a little bit too far.
Speak up, then, let's have your requests.
ALTMEYER: Any old thing. I'm not particular.
(*The holes are all bored now, and plugged.*)
MEPHISTOPHELES: (*With weird gestures.*)
Grapes upon the vine are borne;
the he-goat bears the crumpled horn.
Wine is juice, and vine is wood,
this wooden board gives wine as good.
Deep in Nature's heart we see
her profoundest mystery.   140
Draw your corks now, one! two! three!
TUTTI: (*Pulling out the stoppers and seeing the wines of their choice running into their glasses.*)
Oh, look! A fountain! Oh, so grand, so fair!

MEPHISTOPHELES: Take care not to spill a single drop.

Beware!

TUTTI: (*Singing.*)

'Happy as cannibal chiefs are we,

or as five hundred swine...'

MEPHISTOPHELES: Free men, look at them, they are

well on their way.

FAUST: Then let us be on ours.

MEPHISTOPHELES: One moment. Stay

to witness the ideal revelation

of Mankind as the lowest of Creation.

SIEBEL: (*Drinks carelessly, and spills some wine on the ground where it bursts into flame.*)

Help! Fire! Help! The flames of Hell! 150

MEPHISTOPHELES: Friendly element, be still!

Only a spot of purgatorial flame

this time.

SIEBEL: You'll pay for this before

you leave. What do you take us for?

FROSCH: Just let him try that trick again.

ALTMEYER: Shouldn't we just show him the door?

SIEBEL: Have you the temerity, Sir,

to practise your hocus-pocus here?

MEPHISTOPHELES: Quiet, you fat barrel!

SIEBEL: Broomstick! Are you 160

wanting a quarrel?

BRANDER: We'll whack you blue!

ALTMEYER: (*Draws a bung from the table, and a spurt of fire leaps out.*)

Fire! I'm on fire!

SIEBEL: Witchcraft, in Heaven's name!

Let's get the wretch! An outlaw is fair game!

(*They advance on MEPHISTOPHELES, knives drawn.*)

MEPHISTOPHELES: (*With solemn gestures.*)

Vision, illusion,

bring them confusion,

and this to conclusion!

(*They all stand looking at each other in astonishment.*)

ALTMEYER: Where am I? How did I reach this lovely land?
FROSCH: Vineyards do I see?
SIEBEL: Grapes drop into your hand.
BRANDER: Under this arching, leafy canopy,   170
    what are these vines, what are these grapes I see?
    (*Takes SIEBEL by the nose, the others follow suit, all raising
    their knives.*)
MEPHISTOPHELES: (*Solemnly, as before.*)
    Illusion, take the veil from off their eyes:
    now see the humour of the Lord of Flies.
    (*He vanishes with FAUST. The others let go of each other.*)
SIEBEL: What's this?
ALTMEYER: What's going on?
FROSCH: Was that your nose I held?
BRANDER: Then I must have been holding yours.
ALTMEYER: I felt
    a sort of shock through all my limbs, I swear.
    I think I'm going to faint – get me a chair.
FROSCH: Will someone tell me what it's all about?
SIEBEL: Where is the villain? If I sniff him out,
    he won't leave here alive.
ALTMEYER: I saw him ride   180
    out of the cellar-door, astride
    a barrel – up into the air he rose,
    and passed right overhead.
    My feet feel just like lead.
    (*Going back to the table.*)
    Is there some wine left, d'you suppose?
SIEBEL: All trickery, cheats and lies.
FROSCH   But I still think
    that that was real wine we had to drink.
BRANDER: The grapes were real too, wouldn't you have said?
ALTMEYER: Who says the age of miracles is dead?

5: The witch's kitchen

FAUST: Why have you brought me to this crazy witch?
    Will she do what I want – will I improve?

Cantrips and potions brewed by some mad bitch
are hardly likely – are they? – to remove
thirty years from my age. Dear God, if you
can think of nothing better, what am I to do?
Has neither Nature nor the human mind
yet found a cure of some superior kind?

MEPHISTOPHELES: Well, since you ask, here's Nature's
recipe:
no quacks, no witchcraft, absolutely free. 10
Back to the land with you at once;
dig, delve, hack, cultivate the ground,
confine yourself within the narrowest round,
and be content to be an unthinking dunce.
Support yourself on simple, healthy fare,
live *with* the beasts and *as* a beast. Take care
the fields you reap are spread with your own dung.
And there you have it! Nature's wonder-cure.
At eighty years of age you'll still be young.

FAUST: Though I'm prepared to call a spade a spade, 20
I'm not cut out to use one, I'm afraid.
I was not put on earth to hedge and ditch.

MEPHISTOPHELES: That is why we have come to see
the witch.

FAUST: Why does it have to be this mad old crone?
Can't you brew up the medicines on your own?

MEPHISTOPHELES: The Devil has, I dare say just like you,
things he would rather not know how to do.
Work of this kind requires the strict appliance
of endless patience, just as much as science.
(*Some little long-tailed monkeys, who have been playing with
a large ball, now roll it forward.*)

HE-MONKEY: The world you see 30
rolls ceaselessly
up and down
with a glassy sound
now it cracks wide
nothing inside
see it glitter

71

there still brighter
I'm alive, hear it cry
dear son beware
do not go there   40
or you will die
it's only clay
and crumbles away

FAUST: (*Has meanwhile been gazing into a mirror.*)
Look! In the mirror! Is it possible
a human being could be so beautiful?

MEPHISTOPHELES: Well, naturally, when God created
Woman,
He made a pretty one. He's only human.

WITCH: (*Entering down the chimney with eldritch shrieks.*)
What's to do?
Who are you?
Where are you from?   50
Why have you come?
Hellfire harrow
you to the marrow!

MEPHISTOPHELES: You bag of bones, you gargoyle,
don't you know me?
Down on your knees, show the respect you owe me.
Or must I say my name?

WITCH: My Lord, forgive my being so impolite.
I saw no cloven hoof.

MEPHISTOPHELES: Well, that's all right
this once. It's easy to forget
how long it's been since last we met.   60
The world is getting so sophisticated,
your fire-and-brimstone devil's quite outmoded.
Horns, tails and talons aren't appreciated;
nor is my hoof, my trade-mark, which I just can't lose.
My social life might well be incommoded;
so I am in no position to refuse
the slight assistance of corrective shoes.

WITCH: Really, you could have knocked me flat,
Old Nick himself, and paying me a visit.

MEPHISTOPHELES: Woman, do not call me that. 70
WITCH: It's just a nickname, not an insult, is it?
MEPHISTOPHELES: A fairy-tale is how they now dismiss it.
    And yet, the loss is hardly Mankind's gain.
    The Evil One is dead, the evil ones remain.
    Just call me Baron: that will do.
    The crest on my armorial bearing
    is surely not unknown to you.
    Perhaps it's time it had an airing.
    (*He makes an obscene gesture.*)
WITCH: Ha! Ha! I might have known. The same obscene
    and dirty-minded wretch you've always been. 80
MEPHISTOPHELES: (*To FAUST.*)
    Learn from this conversation, not to pitch
    the jokes too high, when dealing with a witch.
WITCH: Well, gentlemen, what can I get for you?
MEPHISTOPHELES: A glass of your rejuvenating brew.
    But let us have the vintage stuff;
    the new will not be strong enough.
WITCH: You're welcome. There's a bottle on the shelf
    I take a swig from now and then myself.
    But is your friend prepared? You know, if not,
    a drop of this could kill him on the spot. 90
MEPHISTOPHELES: No worries there: my friend is quite
                              immune.
    Give him the best you have. I would be thankful
    if you could start the spells, etcetera, soon:
    and serve the poor man up a good-sized tankful.
    (*The WITCH begins to cast her spells.*)
FAUST: Do we need this outmoded, tasteless stuff?
    I've known that mumbo-jumbo long enough.
    That rubbish is a conjuring-trick, at best,
    and leaves me quite profoundly unimpressed.
MEPHISTOPHELES: It gets a laugh.
FAUST: Well, what the joke is
    I do not know.
MEPHISTOPHELES: Then don't be so strait-laced. 100
    Doctors must have recourse to hocus-pocus,
    or else the whole thing looks too commonplace.

(He motions FAUST into the circle.)

WITCH: This you must know
    make ten from one
    the two let go
    the three add on
    and you are rich
    so speaks the witch
    lose the four
    and add the five 110
    and six to give
    the seven and eight
    so all is straight
    and it is done
    and nine makes one
    and ten is none
    this is the witches' one-by-one.

FAUST: What is this lunatic feefifofum?

MEPHISTOPHELES: Don't worry; there's still quite a lot
                       to come.
    It's all like that: the book's well known to me. 120
    I've lost much time in puzzling over its pages.
    A downright paradox will always be
    a mystery both for fools and solemn sages.
    My friend, the art's both old and new:
    the fashion's still as it used to be.
    By means of three-and-one, and one-and-three,
    error is spread abroad in place of truth.
    Men still teach nonsense, undeterred, in schools.
    People don't bother to dispute with fools.
    Men will think what they hear, however dense, 130
    must somewhere have a basis of good sense.

FAUST: What is this trash she's doing for us?
    My head is splitting: I feel that I
    am listening to a mighty chorus
    of gibbering idiots in full cry.

MEPHISTOPHELES: Incomparable prophetess, enough
    mystification, just dispense the stuff!
    (The WITCH gives FAUST the cup: as he raises it to his lips
    a little flame darts up from it.)

Down it in one! No heeltaps! What? Afraid
of a little fire after the pact *we've* made?
Out of the circle now. You must keep active   140
to let it circulate.
WITCH: Hope it'll be effective.
MEPHISTOPHELES: If there is any way in which I might
    repay you, tell me on Walpurgis Night.
FAUST: Where is the mirror? Let me see
    the beauty that seemed hardly possible.
MEPHISTOPHELES: Come, man, you don't need fantasy.
    I'll fit you with the genuine article.
    With drink like that inside you, every boy's
    Adonis, every girl is Helen of Troy.

6: In the street

FAUST: (*To GRETCHEN, as she passes by.*)
    My fair young lady, may I make so free,
    to offer you my arm and company?
GRETCHEN: Sir, I'm no lady, let alone
    a fair one, and I'll get home on my own.
FAUST: Oh, Heavens, but that girl is beautiful!
    I never saw such loveliness before.
    She looks so modest, virtuous, dutiful,
    with just a touch of sharpness, what is more.
    Her red lips, her bright skin, are things that I
    shall not forget until the day I die.   10
    The way she cast her eyes down as she passed
    struck deep into my heart, and held it fast.
    And the short way that she got rid of me,
    was ravishment bordering on ecstasy!
    (*Enter MEPHISTOPHELES.*)
    Listen, you get that girl for me.
MEPHISTOPHELES: Which one?
FAUST: That one.
MEPHISTOPHELES: Ah. Easier said than done.
    This evening she was at confession.
    I heard the priest grant absolution –
    though she had less than nothing to confess.

I scarcely could believe such blamelessness.   20
I have no power over such as she.
FAUST: Oh, surely now, she's well past puberty.
MEPHISTOPHELES: Quite the Don Juan we're getting,
                                        are we not?
FAUST: Forget the compliments. Unless I've got
    that girl in bed with me by midnight, friend,
    consider our agreement at an end.
MEPHISTOPHELES: Very Parisian! Might I suggest you
                                        quench
    your ardour and stop talking like the French.
    Instead of an immediate consummation,
    savour the pleasures of anticipation.   30
    Pay court to her, like those fictitious stallions
    in all those novels by depraved Italians.
FAUST: I can fall to and eat without the sauce.
MEPHISTOPHELES: Pleasantry, and unpleasantry, aside,
    getting that girl is not a matter of course;
    more like the hardest thing I've ever tried.
    Frontal assault will never win the day:
    we must adopt some more strategic way.
FAUST: Get me something she possesses:
    get me some remembrance of her.   40
    That, at least, won't spurn my kisses.
    I can imagine I'm her lover.
    Get me a present for her, right away!
MEPHISTOPHELES: Presents? So soon?
FAUST: She's coming
                                    back this way.
MEPHISTOPHELES: (*Producing a jewel-case.*)
    I bought these once, against just such a day.
    Although they were originally designed
    to catch somebody else I had in mind.
    Temptations are all very much the same.
    Girls will be girls. A game is still a game.
FAUST: I don't know what to do.
MEPHISTOPHELES: Just leave them there.   50
    Or did you have some future plans to wear
    all that yourself? I break myself in two,
    trying to hook a sweet young girl for you,

and you stand gaping there, as if your next
words would be exposition of some learned text.

7: Evening – a small neat room

GRETCHEN: (*Plaiting and putting her hair up.*)
    I'd give a lot if I could know
    who that gentleman was just now.
    A gentleman he was, that much is clear,
    or else he'd not behave so cavalier.
    How thundery and close it is tonight,
    and yet it's not exactly warm.
    I feel a sort of...I don't know...not right...
    I wish my mother was at home.
    I'm feeling nervous as a cat:
    There's nothing to be frightened at.   10
    (*She sings as she undresses.*)
    'A king of a Northern fastness,
    true to the grave, it's told,
    was left, by his dying mistress,
    a drinking-cup of gold.

    'He knew no greater treasure
    in all his after years,
    yet each time he drank a measure,
    his eyes would fill with tears.

    'At last, his life declining,
    he divided his kingdom up,   20
    all to his heirs assigning,
    all but the golden cup.

    'In the great ancestral castle,
    with his knights of high degree,
    he sat and feasted his vassals
    in his palace by the sea.

    'The old man stood there, drinking
    his life's long, last draught up,
    then, into the ocean flinging
    the sacred golden cup.   30

'He stood and watched it fall, and
fill and sink in the sea,
then he turned his face to the wall, and
never more drank he.'
(*As she opens the press to put her clothes away, her eyes fall
on the jewel-case.*)
What's this? Dear God in Heaven, what do I see?
I never saw such things. They're good enough
for a princess. How would this look on me?
I wonder who can possibly own such stuff?
If only some of them belonged to me,
people would look at me quite differently.   40
What is the use of youth and looks?
All very fine for folk in books,
but no one wants it any more:
their praise has pity at its core.
They just want gold
to have and to hold,
that's all. God help the poor.

8: Taking a walk

FAUST walking up and down, lost in thought.

MEPHISTOPHELES: (*Entering.*)
By pangs of love despised, by Hell, and worse,
if I could think of a more effective curse!
FAUST: What's wrong with you? You seem a little sore.
I never saw you look so glum before.
MEPHISTOPHELES: I'd damn my soul to Hell this very
minute,
were it not for the fact that I'm already in it.
The jewels we left, which that girl should have got,
some pestilential priest has swiped the lot!
She told her mother. Instead of saying: '*Bonne chance!*
you lucky girl!' she has an attack of conscience.   10
She has a nose for sin; you may be sure
she sniffed at once the jewels were not quite pure.
'Gretchen, my girl,' says she, 'ill-gotten wealth

corrupts the mind, it's not good for your health.
So, to be on the safe side, I'll arrange a
gift to the Church, to keep you out of danger.'
Gretchen is pulling quite a face, of course,
thinking, 'Well, there's goodbye to my gift-horse.'
Thinking besides, 'How can he be
wicked if he can leave such things for me?'   20
Off to the priest, however, who takes one
look at the stuff, and says, 'Child, you have done
a Christian deed, which is its own reward.
Only the Church can properly afford
such carriers of moral indigestion.
Ladies, whole countries fall to her in forfeit,
without her ever complaining once of surfeit;
she alone has the stomach, without question.'
With which, he sweeps the whole lot off the board,
as if they had been crumbs swept off a table,   30
and leaves, as soon as he is decently able.
FAUST: And Gretchen?
MEPHISTOPHELES: In an indecisive mood,
    doesn't know what to do, or if she should.
    But she's more curious than she is cross,
    some consolation in her tragic loss.
FAUST: I cannot bear to think of her downcast.
    Get some more jewels, more splendid than the last.
    That box was nothing much to boast about.
MEPHISTOPHELES: No sooner said than done, you think,
                                    no doubt.
FAUST: Just do it!
MEPHISTOPHELES: Yes, Sir; no, Sir; three bags full!   40
    (*FAUST goes out.*)
    A man in love's a pretty kind of fool.
    To please her ladyship, the silly loon
    would mount a ladder to unhook the moon.

9: Neighbour's house

MARTHA: Oh, God forgive my wretched man!
    I doubt, though, if I ever can.

Leaving me here, upon the shelf,
running off to amuse himself.
I never crossed him: God knows, I did love him!
And now he's left: the rank unfairness of him!
He might even be dead. To think of it!
I wish I had the death certificate.

GRETCHEN: Martha!

MARTHA: Gretchen! What's the matter, girl?

GRETCHEN: I can hardly speak, my head's in such a whirl. 10
Another box of jewels has come for me.
I found them in my room. Who can it be
that's leaving them? And these are even more
splendid than the ones I found before.

MARTHA: This time don't go and tell your mother,
or the priest will have it too, just like the other.

GRETCHEN: But Martha, look, just look at me.

MARTHA: You lucky girl!

GRETCHEN: But don't you see
I can't walk out like this, or wear
them in the church, or anywhere. 20

MARTHA: Then just you come and visit me,
and put the jewels on secretly.
Then, come the holidays, there'll be a chance
to show them piece by piece, not all at once:
a necklace here, an ear-ring there. Your mother
won't notice; if she does, we'll spin some tale or other.
(*A knock at the door.*)

GRETCHEN: Oh, God, is that my mother? Go and see.

MARTHA: A stranger. Come in, Sir.

MEPHISTOPHELES: May I make free
to do just that? Forgive the liberty.
(*Stepping back respectfully as he catches sight of GRETCHEN.*)
Is there a Mrs Martha Schwertlein here?

MARTHA: That's me. 30
What can I do for you?

MEPHISTOPHELES: I didn't know
you had distinguished company. I'd better go.
Forgive me bothering you in this way.
I'll call back sometime later in the day.

MARTHA: Distinguished company! Now there's a joke.
    Hey, girl, he thinks you're carriage folk.
GRETCHEN: Oh, no, Sir, these things don't belong to me.
MEPHISTOPHELES: It was in no way just the jewellery.
    She has such presence, such a way
    with her – I'm so glad I can stay.   40
MARTHA: Now, tell me, Sir, what is your business here?
MEPHISTOPHELES: I only wish my news were happier.
    A gloomy start to our first meeting:
    your husband's dead, and sends you greeting.
    Perhaps it might sound better if I said
    Your husband sends you greeting, and he's dead.
GRETCHEN: I never want to fall in love. To know
    the one I loved was dead, would kill me too.
MEPHISTOPHELES: No pleasure without pain – ah, such
                               is Life!
GRETCHEN: Pray Heaven show him mercy – and his wife. 50
MEPHISTOPHELES: A husband here on earth is what
                              you need,
    a pretty girl like you.
GRETCHEN: Oh, no, indeed!
    I'm not in any hurry to be wed.
MEPHISTOPHELES: No husband? Would a lover do instead?
    'The two divinest gifts of Heaven above –
    a pretty woman in the act of Love!'
GRETCHEN: That's not our custom here, I'd have you know.
MEPHISTOPHELES: Custom or not, such things do
                          happen, though.
MARTHA: How did he die?
MEPHISTOPHELES: I stood there as he lay
    on a bed of dirty straw: he passed away   60
    in Christian penitence. 'Ooooh, wretched sinner!'
    (he cried), 'to leave my wife – could I but win her
    forgiveness for my errors here below...'
MARTHA: Poor man – I had forgiven him long ago.
MEPHISTOPHELES: '...though she, God knows, was
                      more to blame than I.'
MARTHA: What? Were his dying words a dirty lie?
MEPHISTOPHELES: Not so. He had prayed fervently
    for wife and children. Heaven heard his prayer.

They boarded, when a few days out to sea,
a Turkish frigate, with the Sultan's gold on board.   70
His bravery attained its due reward;
he claimed a tidy fortune as his share.
MARTHA: Where is it, then? Buried? Where did it go?
MEPHISTOPHELES: Blown to the four winds. Will we
                                            ever know?

One day in Naples, homeless, wandering,
a pretty girl came and took him under her wing:
showed herself such a true and loving friend,
he bore the marks of it right to the end.
MARTHA: You mean that is the only news you bring?
    No messages? No money?
MEPHISTOPHELES: Not a thing.   80
MARTHA: Not even a rotten keepsake? Is that all?
MEPHISTOPHELES: Ah, one request – three hundred
                                    masses for his soul.

If I were in your shoes, I'd wait the year out,
for appearances, but be on the *qui vive*
for someone else, before those shoes can wear out.
MARTHA: I'd never find one like him if I live
    to be a hundred – ah, he was a love:
    it's just that he was always on the move,
    and all that running after foreign women,
    and foreign wine, and dice – that's what did *him* in.   90
MEPHISTOPHELES: But things might still have all gone
                                            well, if he

    had given you a similar degree
    of freedom here at home. Why, I myself
    would have been glad to take you off the shelf.
MARTHA: You're joking, or I might think I'd misheard.
MEPHISTOPHELES: (I'm off before she takes me at my
                                            word.)

    How does your heart react to this, my lass?
GRETCHEN: What do you mean?
MEPHISTOPHELES: *Sancta simplicitas!*
    Ladies, adieu!
GRETCHEN: Goodbye.

MARTHA: Wait! Can you get
    a deposition, a certificate   100
    of where he's buried, when and how he died?
    I like to have these loose ends neatly tied.
    I want to see his name in the *Gazette*.
MEPHISTOPHELES: What two witnesses declare
    is held as valid everywhere.
    Fortunately I have a friend
    who also saw your husband's end,
    and will be glad to speak in court for you.
    May I present him, Madam?
MARTHA: Oh, please, do!

10: Street

FAUST: How are things? What success? Will it be soon?
MEPHISTOPHELES: She will be yours tomorrow afternoon.
FAUST: Good!
MEPHISTOPHELES: But there's something we have got
    to do for them.
FAUST: Favour for favour. What?
MEPHISTOPHELES: Merely to swear on oath, beyond all
                                    doubt,
    we saw her late neighbour's husband's limbs laid out
    in consecrated ground, in Padua.
FAUST: How wise!
    That means a good long journey for us both.
MEPHISTOPHELES: Don't be naif – we simply swear an
                                    oath.
FAUST: Is that your only answer? Telling lies?   10
MEPHISTOPHELES: Oho! A man of probity. Have you
                                    never
    given false evidence in your life? Not ever
    given opinions, unblushingly,
    on God, the world, and all that therein is,
    on Man, and all the knowledge that is his?
    Things you could never know infallibly?
    Look close: you know as much, you must confess,
    of Mr Schwertlein's death: no more – no less.

FAUST: Still full of sophistry, and lying too!
MEPHISTOPHELES: That would depend upon your point
of view. 20

    I take it that this evening you will try
    to fool poor Gretchen, swear that you will die
    unless she yields herself?
FAUST: It would be true!
MEPHISTOPHELES: Dear me, the things that men in
love will do!

11: Garden

FAUST kissing GRETCHEN's hand.

GRETCHEN: You've no need to do that. My hand's so rough
    and ugly, how you can kiss it I don't know.
    I have to work so hard at home, although
    my mother says I never do enough.

❖

MARTHA: So, Sir, you also are a travelling man.
MEPHISTOPHELES: Needs must, when the Devil drives!
    Business and duty rule our lives.
    So many lovely spots we leave with pain.
    Ah, just to find a home, and not to stir!
MARTHA: Careering round the world may suit the young, 10
    but youth won't last for ever. Dark days come,
    and no one wants to die a bachelor.
MEPHISTOPHELES: The prospect is too grim to
contemplate.
MARTHA: Then, Sir, be wise, before it is too late.

❖

GRETCHEN: Yes, out of sight is out of mind:
    but manners come so easily to you.
    You must know hosts of people, who
    would leave me simply miles behind.
FAUST: One look, one word from you is worth
    more than all the cleverness on earth: 20
    and most of that's pretence.

GRETCHEN: How?

FAUST: Do you not
   realise the real worth of what you've got?
   Innocence, simple love, humility,
   should know their value, though they never do.

GRETCHEN: If you will think a little while of me,
   I shall have time enough to think of you.

FAUST: Are you alone a lot?

GRETCHEN: Well, yes: at home
   there always seems so much needs to be done.
   I seem to be on my feet from morn till night.
   Mother insists on having things just right.   30
   Not that we need to scrape for every penny:
   Father left us better off than many.
   The household is quite small: there's just my mother
   and myself. I also have a brother
   who's in the army and been sent abroad.
   I had a little sister I adored:
   but she died.

❖

MARTHA: We women do not have an easy time:
   a bachelor's a real hard nut to crack.

MEPHISTOPHELES: Not if you undertook to see that I'm 40
   steered onto a more congenial track.

MARTHA: Tell me the truth, now, have you never met
   someone you felt attracted to, as yet?

MEPHISTOPHELES: The proverb says: 'A good fire's
                         half man's life:
   the other half's a good bed and a wife.'

MARTHA: I mean, have you never felt the inclination?

MEPHISTOPHELES: I can't complain of under-estimation.
   'Man's love is of Man's life a thing apart,
   'Tis Woman's whole existence.'

MARTHA: Was that clever?
   Has no deep feeling ever stirred your heart?   50

MEPHISTOPHELES: I'm wise enough to know that one
                       should never
   make jokes with women. It was a quotation.

MARTHA: Oh, you don't understand me.
MEPHISTOPHELES: Pardon me,
    one can't mistake your – generosity.

❖

FAUST: So you did know me from the time before?
    Will you forgive the liberty I took?
GRETCHEN: Didn't you see? I hardly dared to look
    at you, I blushed. I felt so strange, the more
    because I thought that you would take for granted
    a girl like me would do just what you wanted.   60
    Yet I was angrier at myself, it's true,
    because I was not angrier with you.
FAUST: I love you.
GRETCHEN: Wait!
    (*She picks a flower and starts pulling off the petals.*)
FAUST: What's that? No, let me see.
GRETCHEN: It's just a game.
FAUST: What game?
GRETCHEN: You'll laugh at me.
FAUST: What are you muttering? My angel love!
GRETCHEN: He loves me – he loves me not – he loves
                         me – not –
    he loves me – not – he loves me – not – he loves me!
FAUST: Yes, he loves you! Do you know
    the meaning of those words?
GRETCHEN: I'm shivering so.
FAUST: Stop shaking. Let the pressure of my hand   70
    tell you the things that no words can express:
    to give oneself up utterly, to feel
    an ecstasy that must be everlasting...
    eternal...for its end would mean despair...
    no ending...ever...ever...

❖

MARTHA: Night's coming on.
MEPHISTOPHELES: It is – we have to go.
MARTHA: I gladly would have asked you both to stay,
    but it's a wicked place, just here about;

as if the folk had nothing else to do,
nothing to think of, for that matter, too,   80
except other folk's business, who goes in or out.
Of course, one tries to be prudent,
though I say it as shouldn't,
but these things have a way
of getting about,
do what you may.
Where are the young ones?
MEPHISTOPHELES: Fluttered over there,
   like butterflies.
MARTHA: He seems to take to her.
MEPHISTOPHELES: And she to him – but isn't that the
                                             way?

12: A summerhouse

GRETCHEN runs in and hides behind the door.

GRETCHEN: He's coming!
FAUST: (*Entering.*)   Where are you? You're teasing
                                             me.
   I've caught you now.
   (*Kissing her.*)
GRETCHEN: Heinrich! I love you so.
   (*MEPHISTOPHELES knocks.*)
FAUST: Who's there?
MEPHISTOPHELES: A friend.
GRETCHEN: A beast!
MEPHISTOPHELES: It's time to go.
MARTHA: It's late.
FAUST: May I not stay?
GRETCHEN: My mother – no.
   Goodbye.
FAUST: If I must really go – goodbye.
MARTHA: Goodbye.
   (*FAUST and MEPHISTOPHELES leave.*)
GRETCHEN: Good Heavens, how can any man
   know all the things that Heinrich can?

My heart melts when he speaks to me.
I'd never dare to disagree.   10
I feel so stupid. I cannot see
just what it is he sees in me.

13: Forest and cavern

FAUST: Transcendent spirit, you have given me all
    I asked you for. All Nature and all Knowledge
    became my province, and I had the power
    to feel it and enjoy it. Nor was it
    a mere cold, curious glance you let me take.
    You let me gaze into Nature's deepest heart,
    as if into the bosom of a friend.
    The ranks of all things living you paraded
    before me, teaching me to recognise
    my kinship with all creatures, in the water   10
    in the quiet thicket, in the air.
    when the storm howls and whistles through the forest,
    and the great trees fall headlong, bringing down
    neighbouring trunks and branches, with a crash
    that echoes round the hills with hollow thunder,
    you shelter me in safety, in a cave,
    and show me to myself, reveal the depths
    and mysteries that lie hidden in my own body.
    Now the bright moon comes up before my eyes,
    bringing me peace; now there float up before me,   20
    out of the rockface and the dew-drenched bushes,
    silvery forms of lost, forgotten worlds,
    soothing the iron discipline of thought.

    But nothing perfect ever comes to Man.
    I see that now. The happiness you gave me,
    which brought me nearer to the gods, has brought me
    in addition, this companion, whom already
    I can no longer do without, however
    impudently and unfeelingly
    he lowers me in my own eyes, and turns   30
    your gifts to dust and ashes, with a word.

He busily fans a hungry fire of lust
inside me for that object of desire.
I stumble from desire to consummation,
in consummation pining for desire.

MEPHISTOPHELES: (*Entering.*)
Do you intend to live like this for ever?
How can such a life appeal to you so long?
Experiment may all be very clever,
but isn't it time now we were moving on?

FAUST: I wish you could find something else to do   40
than interrupt my happiness to torment me.

MEPHISTOPHELES: I'll leave in that case, glad to do so too,
since you have made your mind up to resent me.
what dreary, frigid life, earth-born, earthbound,
would you have led had I not been around?

FAUST: You cannot understand the vital power
I find from wandering in the wilderness:
no, Devil, if you could hazard the merest guess
at it, you'd make sure it was spoiled within the hour.

MEPHISTOPHELES: Of course – a supernatural delight!   50
Lying there in the mountain dew all night,
feeling yourself, 'at one' with earth and sky,
swelling with immanent divinity,
probing earth's core in tense anticipation,
sharing the labour pains of six days of creation,
feeling the pride, the joy – I know not what –
ecstasy of fulfilment overflows the lot.
Old Adam's lost in heavenly contemplation,
Essence is all – the ape is quite forgot –
your new-found powers of deeper penetration   60
bring things – I hardly dare say how – to consummation.
(*A gesture.*)

FAUST: Shame on you!

MEPHISTOPHELES: Really! Now we're quite put out,
and claim the right to cry 'For shame!'
Chaste ears must never hear the name
of what chaste hearts can't do without.
And apropos – she loves you still the same,
sitting at home in melancholy fashion,

wondering wistfully what became
of all that pent-up raging passion.
Instead of playing Lord of Creation here,   70
I think it might not be a bad idea
if the great man would come down from above
and reward the little monkey for her love.
She finds the hours drag on and on,
she stands at the window, looking down,
then up at the clouds scudding over the town:
'O for the wings of a dove', that is her song,
half the night, and all day long.
Now sad, now cheerful – so it goes –
sometimes it seems she has no more tears,   80
then she is calm, or so it appears,
but you are all the love she knows.

FAUST: Snake! Snake!

MEPHISTOPHELES: (It starts to take.)

FAUST: Distance is meaningless: to her adored
    and unforgotten image I have clung.
    I'm jealous of the body of our Lord
    when she accepts the wafer on her tongue.

MEPHISTOPHELES: I envy you – you know how strong
                                        my will is –
    'the two twin roes that feed among the lilies.'

FAUST: Pimp! Pander! Ponce!

MEPHISTOPHELES: P-p-please, such abuse!   90
    The god that fashioned boys and girls displayed
    an understanding of the world's chief trade,
    and made the tools to put to some good use.

FAUST: Where is the happiness of being her lover
    when her own downfall's all I'll ever give her?
    I am the outcast, homeless, wanderer, refugee,
    monster, restless, purposeless,
    plunging like a cataract into the sea,
    hungering for the dark abyss.
    Can't I be satisfied with my own Hell,   100
    or must I take her innocence as well?
    Devil, help me cut short the agony.
    Let what must come, come – and be quick with it.

Put both of us out of our misery;
let us go down together to the pit.
MEPHISTOPHELES: (There now, the fire burns up, he's
                                        on the boil.)
    Despair's for those who see the end beyond doubt.
    Only for blockheads is there no way out.
    Go in and comfort her, you fool.
    Long live the man who can both dare and do!   110
    I expected something more devil-may-care from you.
    The summit of bad taste, I do declare,
    is a devil who knuckles under to despair.

14: Gretchen's room

GRETCHEN: (*Alone at her spinning wheel.*)
    My peace is gone,
    my heart is sore
    I'll find it never,
    nevermore.

    Where he is not,
    my world is all
    a silent grave,
    and turned to gall.

    And my poor head
    is torn apart   10
    by thoughts of him
    who has my heart.

    My peace is gone,
    my heart is sore,
    I'll find it never,
    nevermore.

    I watch at the window
    for him alone:
    and only for him
    I leave my home.   20

    My one and only,
    my North and South –

his step, his bearing,
his eyes, his mouth,

the sound of his voice
a stream of bliss,
the touch of his hand,
and – ah! – his kiss!

My peace is gone,
my heart is sore   30
I'll find it never,
nevermore.

My poor heart races,
to feel him near:
ah! just to clasp him
and hold him here.

And kiss and kiss
again, till I,
under his kisses,
sink and die.   40

15: In Martha's garden

GRETCHEN: Promise me something, Heinrich!
FAUST: (*Entering.*)

                                       If I can.

GRETCHEN: How much does your religion mean to you?
    I know you are a good, kind-hearted man,
    but I don't think your faith is very true.
FAUST: Leave it alone, child! You believe I'm good:
    for those I really love I'd shed my blood.
    Each has a right to pray as he sees fit.
GRETCHEN: But that's not enough: you must believe in it.
FAUST: Must?
GRETCHEN: If only I could make you see the sense:
    you don't even respect the sacraments.   10
FAUST: Oh, I respect them.
GRETCHEN: That's an easy admission.
    When were you last at Mass, or at confession?
    Heinrich, please tell me, do you believe in God?

FAUST: How can a man say he believes or not?
    Ask anyone – from scholar down to priest –
    if they believe. Their answers will consist
    of questions begged, and mockery
    of the questioner.
GRETCHEN: Then you don't believe a word?
FAUST: You misunderstand, my love, or you misheard.
    Who can dare name God,   20
    and say 'He does exist'?
    Or what sane man resist
    the feeling, 'He does not'?
    All-embracing, all-upholding,
    He upholds, embraces, you, me and Himself.
    Look how the vault of Heaven embraces us.
    Is this not the Earth that holds us up?
    Do not the stars shine down with friendly fire?
    Does not all Creation crowd and teem
    into our hearts and minds   30
    weaving eternal mysteries,
    visible and invisible, about us?
    Open your generous heart, and let it be
    flooded with nameless ecstasy –
    then call it what you will –
    Happiness, Heart, Love or God,
    I have no name for it myself.
    Feeling is all. A name is noise and smoke
    clouding the light of Heaven.
GRETCHEN: So the good Father tells us, although he   40
    puts it a little differently.
    Heinrich...that man who goes around with you...
    I hate him.
FAUST: Why?
GRETCHEN: He sends a shudder through
    my every limb, whenever I come near him.
FAUST: Sweetheart, there is no earthly need to fear him.
GRETCHEN: The moment he sets foot in here,
    he looks around him with a sneer.
    It's written clearly on his face;

his heart will never find a place
for friendship. When that man comes through the door,   50
even my love for you becomes unsure.
And when he's here I cannot pray,
and that is eating my heart away.
Heinrich, you feel it too, you know it's so.

FAUST: It's just an antipathy.

GRETCHEN: I must go.
Oh, if only I lived alone!
I should unlock the door to you tonight,
but Mother sleeps so very light,
and if our love were ever known,
she'd kill me.

FAUST: Angel, no more need be said.   60
Take this: pour three drops in a cup
of something she can drink before she goes to bed.
It'll take more than us to wake her up.

GRETCHEN: But are you sure it isn't dangerous?

FAUST: Would I not have said so if it was?

GRETCHEN: What is it that subjects me to your will?
Do what you like with me, I'll love you still.
Already I have done so much for you,
that there seems little more that I can do.
(*She goes out.*)

MEPHISTOPHELES: (*Entering.*)
Well, has your monkey gone?

FAUST: You wretched spy!   70

MEPHISTOPHELES: I merely happened to be passing by.
You transcendental lecher, d'you suppose
that little girl's not got you by the nose?

FAUST: You scum of filth and fire, you abortion!

MEPHISTOPHELES: I merely wished to add a word of
                                        caution.
She didn't take to me, I can't deny.
She senses in me some mysterious force,
suspects me of Satanic intercourse.
Is it – tonight?

FAUST: And what is that to you?

MEPHISTOPHELES: I like to have my bit of pleasure too.   80

16: At the well

LIESCHEN: Heard about Barbara?
GRETCHEN: No.
LIESCHEN: My girl friend thinks
   she's feeding two now, when she eats and drinks.
GRETCHEN: Poor thing!
LIESCHEN: Is that all you have to say?
   While the two of us were kept at work all day,
   and in all night, she was with him, gallivanting,
   dancing, and carrying on, and always wanting
   that something extra – well, she's got that now.
   So no more Lady Muck – not round here, anyhow.
GRETCHEN: But surely he'll ask her to be his wife?
LIESCHEN: How does he know it's his? Not on your life!   10
   He's other fish to fry, the clever lad.
   He's slung his hook.
   (*She goes out.*)
GRETCHEN: That really is too bad.
   Oh, God, the things I used to say,
   when some poor girl had gone astray!
   My tongue could never find a name
   bad enough – for someone else's shame;
   and now, God help me, I am just the same.
   But all that drove me on to it
   was, oh dear God, so good, so sweet.

17: On the ramparts

In a niche, an image of the Mater Dolorosa. GRETCHEN is putting fresh flowers in a vase in front of it.

GRETCHEN: Mary, look down,
   Thou rich in sorrow's crown,
   have pity on my misery.

   With pierced heart
   and bitter smart,
   gazing upon Thy son's last agony.

Thy piteous sighs,
to Heaven rise,
in His and Thy extremity.

Who can see   10
my agony
that cuts me to the bone?

My heart, afflicted,
broken, rejected,
is known to Thee alone.

Wherever now I go,
such woe, such woe, such woe
is here within unspoken.

And when alone, my fears
bring tears, bring tears, bring tears: 20
I know my heart is broken.

The flower-pots in the window
were wet with tears, not dew,
when early in the morning
I picked the flowers for you.

And early in the morning
the sun shone overhead;
but I was up before him,
in misery on my bed.

From shame and death deliver me.   30
Mary, look down,
Thou rich in sorrow's crown,
take pity on my misery.

18: Night – the street in front of Gretchen's door

VALENTINE: Many a drunken crowd I've been in,
  where men would boast about their women,
  describing, with more noise than wit,
  their own particular favourite,
  and toasting them. Meanwhile, I'd lean
  propped on my elbows, in serene

and quiet confidence, until
they had all talked, or drunk, their fill.
Then I'd say, full glass in hand:
'*De gustibus non disputand-*   10
um, but where in all this land'll
you find a girl to hold a candle
to my own sister, Gretchen? There is none.'
Roars of assent, as everyone
agreed she was the flower of womanhood,
shutting the noisy boasters up for good.
And now... Each time her name is spoken,
it's matter for a dirty joke, and
any filthy drunken brute
can call her whore and prostitute.   20
And like a criminal I sit
sweating to hear such talk, but swallowing it.
I'd like to kill them! But even if I tried,
I could not say that one of them had lied.
Who's coming here, so stealthily?
Now there are two of them, I see.
If one is him! By Heaven, I
swear I shall see the coward die.
FAUST: (*Entering.*)
  I feel the darkness clinging to my soul.
MEPHISTOPHELES: And I feel like a tom-cat on the prowl. 30
  A shudder thrills through each limb and vein
  at the thought of the great Walpurgis Night:
  in two days' time it comes around again;
  you know why you stay up then all right.
FAUST: I should have brought her something.
MEPHISTOPHELES: Does it annoy
  you not to have to pay for what you enjoy?
  Now, listen: here's a work of art
  to makes sure of her silly heart.
  (*Sings to the guitar.*)
  'Kitty, say,
  why d'you stay   40
  at break of day
  before your lover's door?

97

Since here you've strayed,
be good, sweet maid,
or I'm afraid,
you'll be a maid no more.

'So have a care,
for once he's there,
it's goodnight, dear;
he'll twist you round his finger.   50
A girl who's wise
withholds the prize
from prying eyes,
until he's put a ring there.'

VALENTINE: (*Coming forward.*)
    You damned pied-piping ratcatcher! Who the devil are you?
    What are you playing at here? Take that and that!
    (*Smashing MEPHISTOPHELES's guitar.*)

MEPHISTOPHELES: There's a good guitar squashed flat.
    Doctor, stick close – do what I tell you to.
    Out with your trusty snickersnee –
    you thrust – I'll parry – follow me.   60

VALENTINE: Then parry that!

MEPHISTOPHELES: Why not?

VALENTINE: That too?

MEPHISTOPHELES: Of course.

VALENTINE: What? Does the Devil
                                      fight for you?

    What's wrong with me? My arm is lamed.

MEPHISTOPHELES: (*To FAUST.*)
    Now strike!

VALENTINE: (*Falls.*)
                Oh, God!

MEPHISTOPHELES: There now, the brute is tamed.
    But now we must be off, and quickly, please:
    the hue and cry is up, and though I flatter
    myself that I can handle the police,
    a capital charge is quite another matter.

MARTHA: Help! Help!

MEPHISTOPHELES: Come quickly!

GRETCHEN: Someone bring a light!

MEPHISTOPHELES: I heard some shouting – has there
                                   been a fight? 70
GRETCHEN: Mother of God – oh, no! A doctor!
MARTHA: Is he dead?
VALENTINE: I'm dying – that is easily said,
    still easier done, I have no doubt whatever.
    Gretchen, if you're not good, at least be clever;
    just don't make such a show of it.
    And let me whisper, furthermore,
    if you're going to be a whore,
    then make a proper go of it.
GRETCHEN: Valentine! God! Am I to blame?
VALENTINE: Let us leave God out of this game. 80
    Unfortunately, what is done is done;
    so carry on as you've begun.
    So far it's only one: why stop at that?
    Quantity's what you should be aiming at.
    After a dozen or so it's not so bad, you
    will hardly notice when the whole town's had you.
    I can foresee a time, and not far hence,
    when every decent citizen will turn
    aside from you, you whore, and spurn
    you like a carrier of pestilence. 90
    Inside you then your heart will fail,
    to see how people look at you and stare.
    There'll be no more gold chains to wear,
    and no more kneeling at the altar rail,
    no fine lace-collars any more,
    no dances, where you can take the floor.
    You'll hide in some foul hole, where you can be
    with other rejects of society.
    And even if there's mercy in the sky,
    you're cursed on earth until the day you die! 100
MARTHA: Just clear your soul to go to your Redeemer.
    Is He disposed to pardon a blasphemer?
VALENTINE: You withered, pimping pander, you,
    if I could get my hands on you,
    that would be quite enough to win
    pardon for every mortal sin.

GRETCHEN: Brother, I never felt such pain!
VALENTINE: I tell you; tears are all in vain.
When you and honour waved goodbye,
that was for me the *coup de grace.*   110
Now, let us end this sorry farce,
and like a soldier, let me die,
and go through everlasting sleep,
my rendezvous with God to keep.
(*He dies.*)

19: Cathedral

Organ and choir. GRETCHEN in the congregation. An Evil Spirit (MEPHISTOPHELES) whispering over her shoulder.

CHOIR: *Dies irae, dies illa...*
MEPHISTOPHELES: What are you praying for? Your
                                    mother's soul?
Your hand prepared the draught that sent it to
its long long sleep of pain.
And on your doorstep, say, whose blood is that?
And just below your heart, is there not something
already quickening into life, and threatening you
with its foreboding presence?
CHOIR: *Quantus tremor est futurus...*
MEPHISTOPHELES: Horror has you   10
the trumpet sounds
the graves are shaken
and your heart
now flares up
from ashen rest
reborn in you
to pangs of flame.
CHOIR: *Tuba mirum spargens sonum...*
GRETCHEN: Oh, to escape!
I feel the music   20
stifling me.
The singing melts
my heart within me.

CHOIR: *Mors stupebit et natura...*
GRETCHEN: I cannot breathe.
    The minster walls
    close in on me.
    The vaulted roof
    is choking me –
    give me some air!   30
CHOIR: *Liber scriptus proferetur...*
MEPHISTOPHELES: Trying to hide?
    Sin and shame
    cannot be hidden.
    Calling for air and light!
    Creature of shame!
CHOIR: *Judex ergo cum sedebit...*
MEPHISTOPHELES: The saints have turned
    their faces away.
    The righteous shudder   40
    to touch your hand.
    Accursed! Accursed!
CHOIR: *Rex tremendae majestatis...*
GRETCHEN: Help! Neighbour! Your smelling salts...
    (*She faints.*)

20: Walpurgis Night

FAUST and MEPHISTOPHELES journeying through the Harz mountains.

MEPHISTOPHELES: Wouldn't you like a broomstick to
                               bestride?
    I wouldn't refuse the randiest goat to ride.
    We're nowhere near the place we're aiming for.
FAUST: As long as I'm still fresh, I need no more
    than a good, stout stick to lean on. And besides,
    what do we gain by shortening the way?
    We thread our passage through the valleys' maze,
    then clamber up the rock-wall's face,
    where the foaming cataract falls in spray:
    this is what makes a traveller's day.   10

Through birches, even firs, now steals the spring:
how can our limbs resist its quickening?
MEPHISTOPHELES: To be quite frank, I haven't felt a thing.
Inside me, it's still winter. I must say
I'd prefer frost and snow along the way.
FAUST/MEPHISTOPHELES/A WILL-O'-THE-WISP:
(*Singing variously.*)
Too-whit, too-whoo: now sounding near,
owl, jaybird, lapwing, all appear;
are all the birds still waking here?
In the thickets, are those lizards
with spindly legs and swollen gizzards?   20
And wondrous roots, like serpents, rise,
coiling out of rock and sand,
grasping out on every hand
to scare us, take us by surprise.
And from rough, inchoate forms
polyp-tentacles spread abroad
toward the traveller. And in swarms,
mice, all colours, horde on horde,
run through moss and heather. Over-
head a myriad glowworms hover,   30
massed, bewildering to the view,
our confusing retinue.

What is happening, can you tell?
Are we moving? Standing still?
All things seem to spin and fly.
Rocks and trees grimace; the great
crowds of will-o'-the-wisps inflate
to monstrous size and multiply.
MEPHISTOPHELES: Doesn't Duke Mammon make a grand
show of his palace, lit up for the occasion?   40
You're lucky to have seen the illumination:
the rowdier guests, I think, are close at hand.
FAUST: The storm-witch hurtles howling through the air:
she beats down savagely on the back of my neck.
MEPHISTOPHELES: Hang on to those ancient ribs of rock,
or she'll hurl you down the precipice. Beware!

Fog thickens the dark:
Listen! the storm cries in the trees.
The owls fly off in fright: and hark!
the pillars of the palaces   50
of evergreen split and crack,
the branches creak and break,
the huge trunks threaten and moan,
the roots upturned, gape and groan;
tangled, confused, and rent they fall,
and dreadful ruin covers all;
while through the wreckage-choked abyss
the furious storm-winds howl and hiss.
Listen! voices! Do you hear?
Above us, far off? Or is it near?   60
Yes! All along the mountain-side,
the witches, singing as they ride.
WITCHES: (*In chorus.*)
The stubble is yellow, the corn is green:
the witches' company is seen.
Over trees and rocks they whirl and float,
farting witch on stinking goat.
WARLOCKS: (*In chorus.*)
The way is wide, the way is long.
How about this for a crazy throng?
The besom scratches, the pitchfork pokes,
the womb bursts open, the infant chokes.   70
VOICES FROM BELOW: We long to be in your company.
We wash behind, before, but we
are barren to all eternity.
WITCHES/WARLOCKS: The winds die down, the stars
                                              grow pale,
the sad moon hides behind her veil.
Careering on, the magic choir
scatters a thousand sparks of fire.
VOICE FROM BELOW: Wait! Wait!
VOICE FROM ABOVE: Who's calling below?
VOICE FROM BELOW: Take me with you, don't leave me
                                      behind! 80
Three hundred years I've been struggling up

and never reached the mountain top,
where I can be with my own kind.
WITCHES: The broomstick bears us, so does the besom,
pitchfork and billy-goat make up a threesome.
He who cannot get here tonight
is damned out of mind and out of sight.
HALF-WITCH: (*Below.*)
I stumble after on feet of lead.
How far the others are ahead!
At home I find no peace nor quiet, 90
and nor will I find it in this riot.
MEPHISTOPHELES: What a crush, what a push, what a
rush, what a babble,
a hissing, squirming, chattering rabble,
sparking, spraying, straining and shitting,
in short, a typical witches' meeting!
Doctor, your hand! In one bound, we are free.
It's too hot even for the likes of me.
FAUST: Spirit of contradiction! I admit
I'd rather be there in the thick of it,
to see why people struggle to be involved 100
with Evil – many problems would be solved.
MEPHISTOPHELES: And just as many started. Let them riot
through the wide world, while we sit here in quiet.
I know a little club where we
shall not be strapped for company.
You'll find young witches there, stripped to the buff,
and old ones – mercifully dressed, if not enough.
Come, show a proper spirit, just for me!
Much sport and little donkey-work: you'll see!
(*To a group of old men sitting round a dying fire.*)
Old clubmen, why are you sitting the party out? 110
I would have thought I'd find you in the rout
of gilded youth, not sitting on your own.
Surely you get enough of that at home?
A GENERAL: Serve your country as you may:
put not your trust in any nation.
People are like women: they
prefer the rising generation.

A MINISTER: The shift away from the Right has reached a
stage

    where one can only mourn the Good Old Days.

    Our word was Law and Order then: our ways   120

    the right ones. Yes, that was the Golden Age.

A PARVENOO: We really knew exactly how to save

    the situation. We did things we shouldn't have.

    Now things have started to go badly wrong,

    because we wanted to hold on too long.

AN AUTHOR: Do people want to read a book today that has

    a grain of sense between its covers? As

    for the so-called rising generation, it's

    a pack of ignorant illiterates.

MEPHISTOPHELES: (*Suddenly appearing very old.*)

    This is my last Walpurgis Night;   130

    for these people Doomsday is in sight.

    My little glass is dry at last,

    the universe is sinking fast.

A HUCKSTER-WITCH: Kind gentlemen, don't pass me by!

    I've nothing here that you can find,

    that hasn't, in its own small way,

    done harm to the world, and to Mankind.

    No dagger here that hasn't tasted blood,

    no vessel here that hasn't poured a flood

    of deadly poison into some strong frame,   140

    no jewel that's not procured some poor girl's shame,

    no sword here that's not been used to attack

    a friend, or stab an enemy in the back.

MEPHISTOPHELES: Grandma; there's no more sale for
things like these:

    all people want these days are novelties.

FAUST: (*Looking into the crowd.*)

    Who is that woman?

MEPHISTOPHELES: Watch her carefully.

    Lilith.

FAUST: Who?

MEPHISTOPHELES: Adam's first wife. Take care

    you do not tangle in her hair;

that is her only ornament, as you see.
When once she takes a young man in that snare,   150
she doesn't let him go so easily.
FAUST: (*Dancing with a YOUNG WITCH.*)
    A lovely dream once came to me:
    I dreamt I saw an apple tree.
    Two apples hung there, glowing bright;
    they led me upward, out of sight.
YOUNG WITCH: I've known the apples tasted nice,
    since long ago, in Paradise.
    I feel so happy now I know
    such apples in my garden grow.
MEPHISTOPHELES: (*Dancing with an OLD WITCH.*)
    A weird dream once came to me: 160
    I dreamt I saw a blasted tree.
    A great big gash ran down the back;
    no joke, but still, a dirty crack.
OLD WITCH: Respectfully I here salute
    His Lordship of the Cloven Foot.
    I hope he's brought a good, thick pole;
    it keeps me happy, on the whole.
MEPHISTOPHELES: (*To FAUST, who has stopped dancing.*)
    Why did you let that pretty creature go?
    I thought that you were all set for an idyll.
FAUST: Well, so I was, and then, right in the middle,   170
    a little red mouse jumped out between her lips.
MEPHISTOPHELES: Complaints, complaints – at least it
                                 wasn't grey.
    You really should not be fussy in this way
    about the details of erotic partnerships.
FAUST: Then I saw...
    (*He breaks off.*)
MEPHISTOPHELES: What?
FAUST: Mephisto, do you see
    that pale girl over there? How slowly she
    moves along, as if here feet were chained.
    Something about her I seem to recognise.
    Could it be Gretchen? Can I believe my eyes?

MEPHISTOPHELES: No more of that! It does no good to
                                   look. Take care! 180
   It's an illusion, lifeless – there is nothing there.
FAUST: The eyes are empty, dead, devoid
   of sense and feeling. And is this
   the face that she held up to kiss?
   Is this the body I enjoyed?
MEPHISTOPHELES: You gullible fool! That is the
                                  witchcraft: she
   makes everybody think it's *their* lover they see.
FAUST: Oh, but such painful love, such loving pain…
   her eyes will never let me go again.
   Look! Round her neck! A single scarlet thread, 190
   thin as a knife-blade.
MEPHISTOPHELES: So there is.
   They say on certain nights she tucks her head
   under her arm. Still chasing fantasies?
   This sort of evening is the natural sphere
   of the gifted amateur, that much is clear.
CHORUS: Drifting cloud and mist recede,
   daylight to discover:
   breezes blow through leaf and reed;
   our long night is over.

21: Gloomy day – open country

FAUST: I am in agony! Despair! That she, so gentle, so
   unhappy, that she should be thrown in prison, to suffer
   like a criminal. And you, you treacherous, misleading
   spirit, you kept it from me, keeping me amused the
   whole time with ridiculous distractions, hiding her
   growing misery from me and leaving her to die without
   assistance.
MEPHISTOPHELES: She's not the first.
FAUST: You hound! You filthy monster! Oh, infinite
   Earth-Spirit, change him back, oh, change the reptile 10
   back into his dog's shape, the one it so amused him to
   assume when scampering ahead of me at night, getting

under the feet of harmless passers-by, and when they fell, sinking his teeth in them. Change him back into his favourite shape, so that he can crawl on his belly in the dirt in front of me, where I can kick him, the despicable creature. Not the first! Oh, grief, grief incomprehensible to the human mind, to think that more than one human creature had to plumb the depths of agony like this, and that his death-throes failed to atone for the sins of all the others, in the eyes of an all-forgiving Heavenly Father. I am pierced to the very soul by one girl's fate, while you grin easily at the doom of thousands.   20

MEPHISTOPHELES: Well, here we are again, at our wit's end: the point where Man's intelligence breaks down. If you were unable to stand the heat, why did you not stay well clear of the kitchen? You want to fly, but have no head for heights. Did we force ourselves on you, or you on us?

FAUST: Save her!   30

MEPHISTOPHELES: Who was it ruined her, you or me?
(*FAUST looks around wildly.*)
Looking for thunderbolts? How fortunate they were not given to poor suffering mortals! Smashing one's innocent critics into pieces: that is the tyrant's method of disposing of all embarrassments.

FAUST: Then take me to her!

MEPHISTOPHELES: And what about the danger to yourself? Remember you're still wanted in this town for murder.

FAUST: Take me where she is, I tell you. Help me set her free. Let us go at once!   40

22: Night – open country

FAUST and MEPHISTOPHELES galloping past on black horses.

FAUST: What's moving around up on Gallows Hill?
MEPHISTOPHELES: I've no idea what they're stewing
                                   and brewing.
FAUST: Swooping, drooping, hopping, stooping.

MEPHISTOPHELES: A witches' coven.
FAUST: They're spreading something. A ritual.
MEPHISTOPHELES: Ride past! Ride fast!

23: Prison

GRETCHEN: (*Singing.*)
    My mother the whore
    she took my life
    my father the thief
    ate me on his knife
    my sister took
    my bones one by one
    and laid me somewhere
    out of the sun
    and so I grew
    the wings of a dove   10
    to fly far away
    to my tr...
    (*Cowering on her bed.*)
    Oh, they are coming. Death is hard, so hard.
FAUST: (*Entering.*)
    Quiet. I have come to set you free.
    (*He takes hold of her chains, to unlock them.*)
GRETCHEN: Go away! It's the middle of the night.
    Couldn't you even wait till it was light?
FAUST: Oh, no!
GRETCHEN: Please let me live, please spare me.
    I'm young, so young, once I was pretty too;
    and that's how I came here.
    My friend was with me; he's not here today.   20
    Look at my wreath, all torn. They threw away
    my flowers. Don't – don't touch me! Did I ever
    do anything to you? I have never
    set eyes on you in my life before.
FAUST: Oh, God, how can I stand this any more?
GRETCHEN: I'm at your mercy now. All right.
    But let me nurse my child just once again.
    I nursed it tenderly all through the night –

to torture me they took it from me; then
they said that I had murdered it. It's gone,   30
and I shan't ever be happy from now on.
They're singing songs about me: I don't know
how people can torture other people so.
(*FAUST throws himself down on the ground. GRETCHEN
follows suit.*)
Yes, let us pray to the saints on bended knee.
Under this flagstone – can you see? –
that's the pit of Hell
where the devils dwell.
Can you hear that voice
making that fearful noise?

FAUST: Gretchen! Gretchen!

GRETCHEN: That was my lover's voice!   40
(*She jumps up. Her chains fall away.*)
Where is he? I heard him call!
'Gretchen!' he called me, and through all
the howling and gnashing of teeth I knew
his voice. Where is he?

FAUST: Here, love.

GRETCHEN: Is it true?
Tell me again.

FAUST: Love, we must get away.
We cannot risk a moment's more delay.
This is our one chance, which we must not miss.

GRETCHEN: Heinrich, have you forgotten how to kiss?
Why, when my arms are round your neck, do I
feel so afraid, when in the days not long gone by,   50
a word, a look from you, and Heaven flooded down
about me, and you'd kiss me till I thought I'd drown?
Kiss me now –
then I'll kiss you.
Oh, your lips are dead and dumb;
what has become of your love?
Who has stolen mine?
(*She turns away from him.*)

FAUST: Follow me, my love, be brave.
I'll give you all the love I have.
Only come with me now. That's all I ask of you.   60

GRETCHEN: (*Turning back.*)

    Is it you, really? Really, is it you?

FAUST: It is. Now come!

GRETCHEN: You free me from my chain

    and take me in your arms again.

    Don't you feel disgust for me?

    Why not? D'you know who you've set free?

FAUST: The stars are fading. We must go.

GRETCHEN: I murdered my mother. Did you know?

    Sent her to The Great Beyond!

    And drowned my baby in the pond.

    Our baby. Yours too. You! I can't believe it yet.   70

    Your hand! It's not a dream. Why is it wet?

    Quick, wipe it dry. I think it's blood.

    What have you done? Put up your sword. Oh, God!

    Please do it. Something's wrong inside my head.

FAUST: Let the dead past bury its dead.

    You're breaking my heart.

GRETCHEN: No! You're the one who has to stay alive,

    of any of us. If you don't survive

    who will there be to see the graves done right?

    See that it's done before tomorrow night.   80

    Give the best place to my mother.

    Next to her put my brother.

    then me a shade – but not too far – to the side.

    And put the baby here – on my right breast:

    there will be no one else to share my rest.

    I used to dream the two of us would be

    buried together for eternity.

    But there's a dream that won't be coming true.

    I feel I have to force myself on you:

    as if you'd cut me out of heart and mind;   90

    yet there you are – you still look good and kind.

FAUST: If you can recognise me, come with me.

GRETCHEN: Come? Where?

FAUST: To freedom. Out into the world.

GRETCHEN: Into the world? No, not for all the world.

    Into my grave, yes.

To meet my death, yes.
I'll go to everlasting sleep,
or I'll not move another step.
You're leaving? Heinrich! Oh, if only I could come with you.
FAUST: You can. You have to try. The door is open. Just go
through. 100
GRETCHEN: I daren't. Besides, escape will do no good.
They're waiting for me, out there in the wood.
They'll get me in the end, do what I may.
FAUST: Then I shall stay.
GRETCHEN: Quick! Quick!
Save your child!
Keep to the path
across the ridge
beside the brook
over the bridge 110
to the wood beyond
left, where the plank is
in the pond.
Catch hold of it
it's trying to get out
it's struggling still.
Save it! Save it!
FAUST: Oh, calm yourself! Think what it is you're saying.
GRETCHEN: If only we could once get past the hill.
My mother sits there on a stone – 120
I feel a chill of dread –
my mother's sitting there on a stone –
she nods and wags her head.
But not in sign to me; her head's too heavy for her.
She won't wake now. She's slept too late. Before, her
sleep made sure that we could be alone.
That was a happy time – and now it's gone.
FAUST: I've used up every prayer and argument:
you're coming with me now, with or without consent.
GRETCHEN: Take your murdering hands off! What are
you trying to do? 130
Time was when all I did was done for love of you.
FAUST: It's daybreak. Oh, my love, my only love.

GRETCHEN: Day? Yes; today. My last day dawns on me;
    my wedding-day, it was supposed to be.
    (Tell no one you've already been with Gretchen.)
    My wreath. What a shame!
    It's faded now.
    We'll meet somehow,
    but not dance again.
    The crowds are gathering out there,   140
    in silence they overflow the square.
    The death-bell tolls, the rod is snapped:
    now they seize me, my wrists are strapped,
    to the scaffold they drag me, violently.
    On his own neck, each man can feel
    the breath and twitch of falling steel.
    Crack! and the world fades, silently.
FAUST: Oh, God in Heaven, why was I ever born?
MEPHISTOPHELES: (*Appearing outside.*)
    You'll wish you hadn't been if you don't come soon.
GRETCHEN: It's him! It's him! Keep him away from me!   150
    I am on holy ground, in sanctuary.
    He's come to claim my soul.
FAUST: No! Live! You must!
GRETCHEN: Judgment of God, in Thee I place my trust.
MEPHISTOPHELES: Come, or I'll leave you with her in
                               the lurch.
GRETCHEN: Father, save me! Holy Mother Church
    protect me! Oh, my Saviour, give Thine
    angels charge over me and mine.
    Heinrich, I shudder now to look at you.
MEPHISTOPHELES: Judgment!
VOICE FROM ABOVE: Atonement!
MEPHISTOPHELES: (*To FAUST.*)
                     Come on, away with you.
    (*He vanishes with FAUST.*)
VOICE: (*From within, dying away.*)
    Heinrich! Heinrich!   160

End of Part One.

PART TWO

ACT ONE

1: A pleasant landscape

FAUST lying on a flowery lawn, exhausted, restless, trying to sleep. Twilight. Spirits hover in a circle around him, graceful and diminutive forms.

ARIEL: (*Singing to the accompaniment of Aeolian harps.*)
When spring flowers drift like rain
covering the face of Nature,
when the fields' returning green
blesses every earthly creature,
small of form, but great of spirit,
elves now fly to bring relief
to good and evil, pitying
every soul in pain or grief.

You who float round his head, propitious elves,
now in your ancient kindness show yourselves.   10
Now soothe the cruel war that tears his heart;
remove the bitter arrows of remorse;
from horrors lived through, purge his inward part.
There are four watches in the night's swift course;
fill them, unresting, with your healing art.
Pillow his head in coolness, tenderly;
in Lethe's dew wash memory away.
His cramped and stiffened limbs will soon be free,
strengthened by sleep to rise and meet the day.
CHORUS: (*Variously.*)
Rock the daylight cares away;   20
seal his eyelids up in peace;
close the iron gates of day;
bid all earthly strivings cease.

Night already has descended,
myriad stars hang in the sky;
over all your dreams suspended,
reigns the moon in majesty.

117

Former joy and pain have vanished,
now the hours are swept away.
Wake now! All your ills are banished.   30
Trust the newly-risen day.

Break the brittle husk of sleep.
Greet your hour of destiny.
Speed and wisdom hold the key.
The world is yours to grasp and keep.
(*A tremendous noise heralds the approach of the sun.*)

ARIEL: Hark! The storm of sunrise nears,
signalling to immortal ears
that the new-sprung day appears.
Gates of marble gape asunder
as the sun-car wheels in thunder;   40
music glows and daylight sings;
light is melted into sound;
sight is deafened, hearing blind.
Hear not these unheard-of things!

FAUST: The throbbing pulse of life returns to greet
the dawn of day. The constant earth, all through
the long, dark night, was true to me: it too
breathes with new-quickened life beneath my feet,
and rouses in me the resolve to do
all Man can do to make his life complete.   50
Now the world lies spread open to the day;
the forest hums with multitudinous voice;
light's fingers probe the darkness, from the sky,
and all the myriad forms of life rejoice.
Colour on colour separates from grey,
and all around me here is Paradise.

Look upward now! Already each mountain height
heralds the solemn hour of dawning day;
they are touched first by the eternal light
that only later comes to us below.   60
But now the Alpine slopes are green and bright;
new clarity, new brilliance starts to show,
step by step, over all the countryside.

The sun strides out! – and, blinded by the glow,
my eyes shot through with pain, I turn aside.

So is it, when a long-held hope aspires,
trusting, to the goal of its desires,
and finds fulfilment's door stands open wide;
when suddenly, from the eternal depths inside
an overpowering flame roars to confound us.   70
We wished to light the torch of Life – and look!
a sea of fire – such fire! – washes all round us.
A fire of love? of hate? Both now surround us
in giant sweeping tides of pleasure and pain,
so that we look down to the earth again,
to shelter in youth's, Spring's, everlasting cloak.

Then let the sun stay always at my back!
Down precipices roars the cataract.
I watch it, with growing wonder and delight,
crashing from fall to fall, to join and split   80
in a thousand torrents, hurling up spray and foam,
and suddenly, nobly, rising from the storm,
the rainbow bends, in colours ever-shifting,
now clear and bright, then in the heat-haze, drifting
to spread its fragrant coolness everywhere.
There is the metaphor for the human story:
reflected on, the meaning's crystal-clear;
our life is brilliant, but reflected glory.

2: Throne-room of the Imperial Palace

EMPEROR: Greetings to all men over whom I rule!
    The wise men are all here – but where's my fool?
COURTIER: He fell downstairs the other day.
EMPEROR: Dead or just drunk?
COURTIER: Ah, Highness, who can say?
SECOND COURTIER: Another came, with lightning speed,
    to fill the vacancy at need.
    His clothes are rich, but so bizarre,
    that people simply stand and stare.

The guards detained him – though I see
somewhat inefficiently.   10
MEPHISTOPHELES: (*Entering.*)
Who is abused but gladly hailed?
Who is accepted and rejected?
Who is continually protected?
Who is continually reviled?
Who do you dare not summon here?
Who lives in an exile of his own?
Whose is the name all want to hear?
Who is it kneels before your throne?
EMPEROR: Friend, your material is somewhat flat.
Riddling is these gentlemen's affair.   20
So use your ingenuity on that.
My old fool's gone too far at last, I fear,
so take his place and sit beside me here.
COURTIERS: Another fool – Here we go again –
Where's he come from? – How did he get in? –
The old one came a mighty cropper –
He was a winebarrel – This one's the stopper.
EMPEROR: Why, at a time of general celebration,
need we be bored with problems of the nation?
Irksome at any time, now most of all,   30
because they interrupt the carnival.
But if you think we must, we must indeed.
To business, gentlemen, let us proceed!
CHANCELLOR: Your Majesty alone can exercise
the justice all men rightly love and prize.
But what is the use of intellect,
goodness of heart, the instinct to protect
when immorality stalks through the land,
and mischief hatches mischief on every hand?

They rustle cattle, steal each other's wives.   40
They even lay hands on Church property,
and they get off without a scratch, scot-free,
to boast of it the rest of their vile lives.
Meanwhile the courts are crammed to suffocation
with new, unnecessary litigation,

and outside there is public agitation.
Any accused that has a friend at court
will be acquitted of the worst offence.
But 'Guilty!' is the immediate retort
where Innocence undertakes its own defence.   50
The honest man may, for a time,
fight the corruption, but, at last, he yields:
the judge who's powerless to punish crime
is much worse than the criminal he shields.
A court in which no one can trust, is
no place to go seeking justice.
I paint things black, but would have been
glad not to have described the scene.
(*Pause.*)
Strong measures must be put *in* hand
before the situation's *out* of hand.   60
Your Majesty must authorise reform.
Where all men both inflict and suffer harm,
even the monarchy's no longer safe.
GENERAL: Days of disorder and insanity!
'Kill *and* be killed' is how it looks to me.
As for obeying orders, all are deaf.
The bourgeois hide behind the city wall,
the upper classes in their armed redoubt;
while holding on to their own power, they all
conspire against us, swear they'll see us out.   70
Meanwhile the mercenaries are growing
mutinous for food and pay;
if they hadn't money owing
they'd be off this very day.
Forbid them what they all want or expect,
and you've stirred up a hornet's nest.
The Empire which they should protect
lies helpless, plundered and oppressed.
Their violence is allowed to rage, unchecked:
already half the world is ruined, wrecked.   80
There are still monarchies abroad, but they appear
to think all this is none of their affair.

TREASURER: Let's not waste time on the *entente*.
    What happened, then, to those much vaunt-
    ed subsidies of theirs, which never seemed to reach us?
    All through the territories at home,
    Your Majesty's possessions have become
    the looted property of other creatures.
    So many old prerogatives are thrown
    away, you've no rights left to call your own.   90
    As for the parties, they – for all they say or do –
    are no more different than a right- or left-hand shoe.
    The people have no further confidence
    in spectacles of mutual incompetence.
    So each man bars his door, puts up the boards,
    and hides away, and scrimps and saves and hoards.
    No money's coming in from anywhere.
    The Treasury is void. The cupboard, Sire, is bare.
STEWARD: To crown all this, Your Majesty, the wine
    is running out – and through no fault of mine.   100
    It's all those swilling young aristocrats,
    who specialise in emptying the vats
    as fast as they are filled. They seem unable
    to stop until they're underneath the table.
EMPEROR: Well, fool, won't you add your stone to the cairn?
MEPHISTOPHELES: No, Sire: look around. You can discern
    the power of Your Majesty. What can fail,
    when Your Majesty's very glance makes strong men quail?
    No accident that Fate has yet designed
    can crush your iron will and noble mind.   110
COURTIERS: He is a rogue – He understands –
    He's lying well – To serve his ends –
    I see his game – Things aren't all they seem –
    What next? – I wonder – Some devious scheme.
MEPHISTOPHELES: Where on earth is there *not* some deficit
    of this or that? In our case, gold is it.
    Of course, you can't just pick it off the floor,
    but insight may detect a hidden store.
    In mountain-veins, in caverns underground,
    gold, raw or minted, can be found, or mined.   120

Who'll find it? Anyone prepared to seize on
the Force of Nature and the Power of Reason.
CHANCELLOR: Nature? Reason? Godlessness!
  Heretics have been burned for less.
  Nature means Sin, and Reason means the Devil;
  between them they engender Doubt,
  a misbegotten, evil, hermaphrodite.
  Not so with us! The Empire is kept free
  from that foul evil, by the alliance
  of Church and Aristocracy,   130
  in combination to save the Nation
  from the insidious march of Science,
  and every similar heresy.
  The rabble-rouser's politics
  allow the rise of an opposition
  of witch-doctors and heretics,
  who lead the country to perdition.
  And now you want to let such people in?
  It's true – a fool's a radical's next-of-kin.
MEPHISTOPHELES: I see you are one of those learned men: 140
  what you can't touch lies miles beyond your ken;
  what you can't grasp does not exist for you;
  what you can't calculate cannot be true;
  what you can't weigh cannot have any weight;
  what you can't coin, it must be counterfeit.
EMPEROR: None of this helps, however, to remove
  our problem. What was that sermon meant to prove?
  I'm bored with this eternal When and How:
  we need gold? Good! Then get it – Here and Now!
MEPHISTOPHELES: I can do that, and more: easy enough,   150
  the task is simple, though the work is hard.
  The gold is there: but how to get the stuff?
  That is the trick – and who knows where to start?
  Here is the point: in periods of invasion
  and foreign armies, men, in desperation,
  have buried their most valuable possessions.
  People have always done so, and they still
  do so unthinkingly; that is, until
  today. Quiet, underground, lies wealth untold:

the land's Your Majesty's – so is the gold! 160
In the event of counter-claimants, he's a
traitor who will not render unto Caesar.
TREASURER: That, for a fool, is no bad point of view.
It is the Crown's established right and due.
CHANCELLOR: Satan is spreading golden snares
to catch the sinner unawares!
STEWARD: In our position, if he gets the gold, the fact is
we can't afford to mind some trivial malpractice.
GENERAL: Shrewd fool! To promise what we all desire.
And where it comes from, soldiers don't inquire. 170
COURTIERS: Two rascals – Both crafty, you can tell –
Dreamer and fool – And so near the throne as well –
The old, old song – The usual question –
The sage speaks at the fool's suggestion.
ASTROLOGER: (*Speaking, prompted by MEPHISTOPHELES.*)
Great Sol himself is pure gold; Mercury,
the messenger, labours for his golden pay;
while Madame Venus practises her wiles on you –
(you all submit the moment that she smiles on you);
chaste Luna's humour changes by the hour;
Mars, even when he sleeps, has threatening power; 180
and Jupiter's still the fairest in the sky;
Saturn is great, though small to the naked eye;
metal he is, but only lightly prized,
his worth being small proportionate to his size.
Ah! but when Sol to Luna is allied,
silver to gold, the world is open wide,
all follows suit; Man wins all that he seeks,
palaces, parks, soft breasts and rosy cheeks.
All these things can be won by the learned man,
who can accomplish what no other can. 190
COURTIERS: What is all this? – It's meaningless –
Quackery – And alchemy –
Too often heard – Don't believe a word –
Deceiving folks – It's all a hoax.
MEPHISTOPHELES: They cannot trust the great discovery;
they just stand in astonishment, and tell

stories of mandrake roots and sorcery,
and old-wives' legends of the Hound of Hell.
What matter if this one denounces witches,
and that one flaunts his wit, if soon   200
his feet develop painful stitches,
and his sure footing lets him down?
COURTIERS: My feet are suddenly like lead –
A touch of gout? – My arm's gone dead –
My big toe has begun to ache
I've shooting pains all down my back –
All indications we could be
standing on a treasury.
EMPEROR: If there is any truth in what you say,
I'll lay down orb and sceptre on the spot   210
and spit on the royal palms; if there is not,
I'll send you packing down to Hell.
MEPHISTOPHELES: Thanks – I already know the way
quite well.
EMPEROR: First I declare a Carnival day of rest:
distracted minds are never at their best.
(*The COURT leaves.*)
MEPHISTOPHELES: These idiots have never learned
that Luck is something to be earned.
Give them the Stone of Wisdom, and you'd find
wisdom would vanish – the stone be left behind.
DRUNKARD: (*Maudlin.*)
Nothing can disturb my pleasure   220
not today, I feel so free;
happiness in tuneful measure,
that's what I have brought with me.
And I keep on drinking, drinking,
come! drink up there! glasses clinking,
at the back there, everyone!
Raise your glasses, drink it down.

Though my wife gave me a ragging,
sneering at my motley coat,
took me down a peg for bragging,   230
called me 'fool' and 'drunken goat';
still I kept on drinking, drinking,

125

kept the beaded bubbles winking;
fools and drunken goats, come on!
Raise your glasses, drink it down.

Let them call me addle-headed:
here's where I shall spend my life.
If the landlord won't give credit,
try the daughter or the wife.
And just keep on drinking, drinking, 240
clink your glasses till you're stinking,
everyone to everyone,
that is how things should be done.

Here and now I satisfy
pleasures that come to my hand.
Where I fall, there let me lie,
since I can no longer stand.
Brothers, keep on drinking, drinking,
keep those glasses clinking, clinking.
I shall meet you all anon, 250
under the table, where I've gone.
FEAR: Through the rout and riot weaving,
torches cast a murky light;
but among all these deceiving
faces, fetters hold me tight.
Go, you idle laughers, scorners,
I mistrust your senseless grin:
all my enemies lurk in corners
here tonight, to fence me in.

Look! a friend comes to betray now, 260
but straight through his mask I see:
recognised, he creeps away now,
though he came to murder me.

I hunger, all my waking hours,
to fly into the world outside;
but overhead, destruction lours.
Doubt and Horror hold me tied.
HOPE: Sisters, today and yesterday
you have been merry, but I know the way

things are with you: tomorrow, masks   270
are thrown aside, and if the light
of torches brought no special pleasure,
we may discover all we ask
in daylight. Singly or together
we shall wander with delight
over lawns, and take our leisure,
work at will, live free from care,
want for nothing, keep aspiring
to the goals of our desiring,
be accepted everywhere,   280
knowing, as a welcome guest,
somewhere we must find the best.

PRUDENCE: (*Leading an elephant.*)
Fear and Hope, now led in fetters,
foes by which men were enslaved,
now they are made harmless. Let us
clear the way there! You are saved!

Here I lead this living mountain,
tower-bearing Behemoth,
unfatigued and steady, mounting,
step by step its dizzy path.   290

Wings of speed and power unfolding,
from the battlements on high,
the goddess turns her gaze, beholding
all her widespread territory.

Fame surrounds her, blazing, glorious,
shines to dazzle all men's eyes:
and her chosen name, Victorious,
Goddess of Man's enterprise.

DRUNKARD: A chariot is swinging through the crowd,
but touching no one – the people don't divide.   300
It shines out like the pictures that they throw
onto the wall at a magic-lantern show.
It's coming on, right at me, out of nowhere –
I've had enough of this. I'm going!

BOY CHARIOTEER: Whoa there!

127

DRUNKARD: Who is this creature then, half-man, half-boy,
    but still the sort that women might enjoy:
    with every promise he'll grow up to be
    a proper little source of misery.
    And who's the stately joker on the throne?
BOY CHARIOTEER: Plutus, the God of Riches. He has come 310
    on a ceremonial visit of state,
    hearing the Emperor's need of him was great.
DRUNKARD: And who, could you inform me, might you be?
BOY CHARIOTEER: Poetry and prodigality,
    the beauty that is superfluity.
    The poet, rich in genius, tends
    more to perfection, the more of it he spends.
    I too am master of a treasure, which is
    more than the equal of King Plutus' riches.
    I dance attendance at his side, 320
    and what he's lacking, I provide.
    (*To PLUTUS.*)
    The truth! For did not you confide
    the whirlwind of the chariot-ride
    to me? You pointed – we are here.
    Often have I flown fearless through the air
    to snatch the palm of Victory for you.
PLUTUS: If you want a certificate of merit,
    then gladly – you are spirit of my spirit.
    Your acts are all extensions of my will;
    if I am rich, then you are richer still. 330
    I value, be it said to your renown,
    the poet's laurel more than any other crown.
    I here declare, in front of everyone,
    we are well pleased in our beloved son.
WOMEN: I'd take my bible-oath that fat one's
    a charlatan – But who is that one
    standing behind him? – He's all skin and bone –
    Kings always have to have a clown –
    Looks like a good square meal is what he'd need –
    Prick him and you'd think he'd hardly bleed. 340
MEPHISTOPHELES: (*As Starveling.*)
    Stand back from me, disgusting female sex!

Good for nothing but to nag and vex.
When you kept house, in days gone by,
Thrift was the name you knew me by.
Then all went well. You could be sure
income exceeded expenditure.
I watched the coffers like a tiger;
no such thing as being too eager.
But following the modern drift,
women have no more use for thrift.   350
They run up bills and then they welsh,
having far more wants than wealth.
Worry is all the husband gets;
on all sides, all he sees is debts.
Meanwhile, his good wife's sole concern,
is to spend all the money she can earn
upon her back...upon her back The crew
of clients wine and dine her better too.
The charm of Gold is heightened by all this.
Now, male in gender, I'm called Avarice.   360
LEADER OF THE WOMEN: Let dragons make dragons'
economies:
    in the end it's only cheats and lies.
    Coming here to teach men to be more
    trouble to us than they were before.
WOMEN: (*Variously.*)
    How could they be more? – The fool
    didn't learn enough at school –
    Pull him down – Thrash the clown –
    Teach the scarecrow to grimace
    on the other side of his ugly face.
PLUTUS: (*To the BOY CHARIOTEER.*)
    Now your heavy duty's finished here,   370
    you are free to go back to your proper sphere:
    this is not it – surrounded by grotesque
    rapacious creatures in wild arabesque.
    Fly to create a private, lonely space,
    where your own beauty may look clear on Beauty's face,
    where Goodness, Truth and Beauty all may be
    your own. Now to the elements be free.

BOY CHARIOTEER: I'll be a worthy envoy of
    the relative whom I most love.
    Where you are is affluence,   380
    where I am, the influence
    of Beauty – Life's inconsistency
    forces Mankind to choose, now you, now me.
    Your devotees enjoy uncounted idle hours;
    mine, the unceasing turmoil of creative powers.
    My influence cannot be concealed:
    where I so much as breathe, it is revealed.
    Farewell – you do not grudge me what I have to do;
    but only whisper, and I shall return to you.
    (*He goes as he came.*)
PLUTUS: The time has come to set the treasure free.   390
    Open the vaults! The gates swing wide – and see!
    The rain of gold descends that will maintain
    the equilibrium of the Emperor's reign.
VOICES FROM THE CROWD:
    Yes! – Look there! – Look here! – The treasure fills
    the coffer to the brim, and overspills –
    Golden vessels melt – And coins, new-fired,
    roll everywhere – It's all my heart desired –
    The chance is offered; take it while you can.
    Just bend down, and rise up a wealthy man.
    Meanwhile the rest of us, quick as lightning flash,   400
    will sequestrate the coffer with the cash.
HERALD: What is the matter, you witless folk?
    It's nothing but a carnival joke.
    Your lust is over for the day;
    d'you think we'd give real gold away?
    For you, in such a crass charade,
    brass farthings would be over-paid.
    Blockheads! You simply can't perceive
    the difference between truth and make-believe.
    Plutus, Lord of Carnival Night,   410
    get this pack out of my sight.
PLUTUS: (*Taking the HERALD's staff.*)
    Maskers, beware the fiery powers
    within this wand, that throws out showers

of sputtering, flashing sparks. Red-hot
it glows already now. Do not
approach too near, or you will be
singed and scorched quite ruthlessly.
Now I begin my circuit round.

CRIES AND TUMULT: We are undone! – Make way! –
                             Give ground! –
  All who can, escape from here! –   420
  Room at the back there! – Give me air! –
  Right in my face it scorched, red-hot –
  I felt the weight of the fiery rod –
  All of us are quite undone –
  Back, back, you milling, masking throng! –
  Back, back, you blocks, you senseless things! –
  Oh, for a pair of good strong wings!

AVARICE: Now we may pleasantly peruse
  this pretty circle, if we choose.
  Women will always take the lead   430
  when it's a matter of gossip or greed.
  My senses aren't completely rusty yet;
  a pretty woman still appeals to me,
  and today, since it's absolutely free,
  let's play the market, see what we can get.
  But with the place so crowded over-full,
  not every word is always audible:
  so let me try – I hope with some success –
  to use some clever pantomime to express
  my meaning. But mere gestures won't suffice: 440
  I need to fabricate some fresh device.
  I'll work the gold in shapes like moistened clay:
  this metal can be worked in any way.

HERALD: What does the skinny fool mean to do,
  kneading the mass of gold like dough?
  However he may press and squeeze,
  he just creates deformities.
  He turns to the women there, but they
  all scream, and make to run away,
  with gestures of disgust. But he   450
  looks ripe for every sort of villainy.

I fear he's happiest when he
offends most against decency.
I can't bear this in silence any more:
give me my staff – I'll drive him out the door.
PLUTUS: He little knows what threatens from without:
    let him indulge his tricks a little longer.
    His time for pranks is quickly running out.
    Law may be strong, but Need is something stronger.
CHORUS OF NYMPHS: (*Surrounding the great god Pan.*)
    See, he is come!   460
    the human sum
    incorporate
    in Pan the Great!
    Spirits of utmost joy, surround him,
    in agile, swaying dance around him.
    Since he is grave, since he is kind,
    joy everywhere he looks to find.
    Under the heavens' azure arch,
    his eyes keep their unresting watch.
    Yet he is lulled by rustling streams,   470
    and breezes cradle him in dreams.
    And when at noon he takes his ease,
    the leaves are silent in the trees,
    and herbs breathe perfume everywhere
    through the still and silent air.
    Then the nymphs, no more a band
    of revellers, sleep where they stand.
    But when, all unexpectedly,
    the great voice sounds, with crashing din,
    like thunder, or the raging sea,   480
    then no man knows what world he's in.
    Brave armies panic in the field,
    and heroes in the tumult yield.
    So Honour him, to whom all Honour's due.
    All hail to him, that led us here to you!
HERALD: But what is the rumour that I hear,
    in every mouth, and every ear?
    Oh, blackest night of suffering,
    what is this evil news you bring?

The coming day will bring, I fear,   490
tidings that none will want to hear.
On every side I hear the cries:
'The Emperor suffers agonies!'
If only it could prove untrue –
the Emperor and his retinue,
on fire! A curse on those who forced
the pitch-soaked garlands on him, brought
him rioting here, till all was caught
in a universal holocaust!
O youth! Youth! Will it never learn   500
that pleasure has its place and hour:
Your Majesty! use, in your turn,
reason alongside absolute power.

Already the forest is on fire;
like tongues, the flames lick higher and higher,
till on the roof the fire plays,
threatening a universal blaze.
Our cup of suffering runs over,
and where salvation is, none can discover.
The Imperial power, that shone so bright,   510
the ash-heap of a single night.
PLUTUS: Long enough has terror reigned;
by my power it shall be restrained.
Strike with the staff upon the ground,
to make it tremble and resound.
Come, mists and heavy clouds, and fall
in gentle rain, to extinguish all,
and make of this tumultuous blaze,
the lightning of soft summer days.
If spirits threaten us with harm,   520
Magic must be used to charm.

3: Pleasure-garden

CHANCELLOR: Your Majesty, in all my days, I never
    thought I would have such welcome news to deliver.
The National Debt has all been paid,

the money-lenders' demands allayed.
I'm freed from such infernal care,
I couldn't be happier anywhere.
GENERAL: My soldiers have been paid: that meant a
siege at the recruiting centres.
It's put some stiffening in the men:
so whores and landlords can breathe again.   10
TREASURER: (*Brandishing a bank-note.*)
And here's the mighty instrument that did it;
which opened up immeasurable credit!
'The Imperial Bank here guarantees to pay
the bearer on demand as follows:
the sum of one hundred thousand thalers,
redeemable at any day.
Delivered under the Imperial Hand.'
The guarantee's under the Imperial land.
EMPEROR: (*Inspecting the note.*)
Which of you has forged our signature?
CHANCELLOR: It is quite genuine, Sire, you may be sure.   20
Recall, Sire, when, last night, as Great God Pan,
Your Majesty appeared, how we proposed the plan
of how the nation, at Your Majesty's will,
might be transformed by a few strokes of the quill.
TREASURER: You signed forthwith, and then, by dint
of dedicated shift-work at the Imperial Mint,
we printed the whole series, overnight,
getting them to the exchanges by first light.
CHANCELLOR: You can't conceive the difference it's made,
calming the people and reviving trade.   30
EMPEROR: This passes for real money, did you say?
At court, in camp, they take this for full pay?
I must endorse it, though I'm mystified.
TREASURER: We couldn't call them in now if we tried.
Once issued, they were snapped up in a flash,
and honoured everywhere, like ready cash.
No need of cumbersome and heavy coins –
the bank-note has disposed of that annoyance.
Through every walk of life it circulates,
the faster, the more profit it creates.   40

The flow of commerce seems to have no end,
as long as their motto continues: 'Spend! Spend! Spend!'
I'd also mention one advantage of it:
a good proportion is Your Majesty's profit.
MEPHISTOPHELES: Such paper, in the place of actual gold,
is practical: we know just what we hold.
The greater part of the treasure is to be found,
throughout your kingdom, untouched, underground
the natural resources of the nation,
beyond both reckoning and imagination.   50
But wise men will, when they have studied it,
place infinite trust in what is infinite.
EMPEROR: Your services deserve to be rewarded,
and so they shall be, now we can afford it.
What happy Fortune brought you to our sight,
as if you'd stepped out of an Arabian night?
Though what you did was noticeably harder
than the mere tale-spinning of Scheherazade.
If in invention too you are her equal,
I wait with some impatience for the sequel.   60
Stay close: the daily round, the common task,
furnish much less than all I need to ask.
I should be grateful for your company:
the world of day-to-day depresses me.
TREASURER: No strife of any kind must mar the alliance
between us and this singular man of science.
(*The EMPEROR and the COURT leave.*)
FOOL: (*To FAUST.*)
Sir, I could use some largesse, don't you think?
FAUST: No, I do not. You'd spend it all on drink.
FOOL: The magic money... I don't understand it.
FAUST: That is because you don't know how to spend it.   70
FOOL: They're falling everywhere. I don't know what to do.
FAUST: Just pick them up. I can't do everything for you.
(*He goes out.*)
FOOL: Look at it all – just waiting to be collected.
MEPHISTOPHELES: You walking vat, have you been
                                    resurrected?
FOOL: Time and again – but this is the best one yet.

135

MEPHISTOPHELES: I see excess joy overflows in sweat.
FOOL: But tell me, look – is this as good as gold?
MEPHISTOPHELES: It'll buy more than your pig's guts
will hold.
FOOL: Could it buy me a farm, or an estate?
MEPHISTOPHELES: By all means. What you bid for, you
will get. 80
FOOL: A country house, with huntin', shootin', fishin'?
MEPHISTOPHELES: And a socially impeccable position.
FOOL: I'll go to bed a landowner tonight!
MEPHISTOPHELES: And now who says that fools are
never right?

4: A gloomy gallery

FAUST: (*To MEPHISTOPHELES.*)
Be quiet – your outworn style of dialogue
gets on my nerves. You do it now to fog
my mind, and to evade my questions.
Well, now I need some really shrewd suggestions.
The Emperor has hinted, no, declared he wants to see
Helen of Troy and Paris, conjured up by me.
The man and woman of the Classical Ideal;
he wants to see them, large as life, and just as real.
Put your mind to it. I dare not break my word.
MEPHISTOPHELES: To give it in the first place was absurd. 10
FAUST: Comrade! I don't believe you've ever thought a
scrap about where your cleverness has brought us.
We've made the Emperor rich, and now
he has to be amused, and this is how.
MEPHISTOPHELES: You think one pulls such things out
of the blue?
A case of 'Whistle and she'll come to you'?
In the same way we made the paper money?
Calling up old Greek heroines isn't funny.
Pre-Christian spirits are not my affair;
they have their own particular Hell somewhere. 20
Still, there are ways...
FAUST: Then tell me what they are.

MEPHISTOPHELES: The Mothers.
FAUST: Mothers?
MEPHISTOPHELES: That word – does it jar?
FAUST: The Mothers.
MEPHISTOPHELES: The Mothers.
FAUST: No, it just sounded strange.
MEPHISTOPHELES: Strange is the word – goddesses,
                                        out of range
   of Space and Time, unknown to human mind,
   and named reluctantly, even by our kind.
FAUST: Show me the way to them.
MEPHISTOPHELES: There is no way.
   A way to the Unreachable you cannot reach:
   the Unbeseechable, you cannot beseech.
   No locks or bolts or bars for you to pass,   30
   just utter solitude, of a different class
   from all you've ever known. Are you prepared?
FAUST: It will take more than that to make me scared.
   Such speeches put me in mind of earlier days,
   when I learned emptiness, and taught it too.
   When I spoke out for the truth, and tried
   to interpret it, I was attacked in ways
   that drove me into solitude, where I
   despaired of company – until I pitched on you.
MEPHISTOPHELES: What you see as the enormousness
                                        of Space, 40
   is circumscribed by a firm sense of Place.
   Your universe has stars and suns; the sea,
   though vast, is made of water you can see.
   But there, there will be Nothing, there will be
   nothing to hear, to feel, to smell, to see.
   In the dark emptiness of the Eternal Void,
   thought works alone – the senses are destroyed.
FAUST: The mystic teacher usually delights
   in humbugging his luckless neophytes.
   This time, things are reversed: I am employed   50
   to bring *you* back new wisdom from the void.
   Like the cat in the fable, you use me to
   claw chestnuts out of the fire for you.

So be it then! In what you call
the Nothing, I may find the All.
MEPHISTOPHELES: My compliments, on parting: I can tell
you really know your Devil very well.
Here is the key.
FAUST: A little thing like that?
MEPHISTOPHELES: Hold it before you under-estimate.
FAUST: It's growing, glowing, sparkling in my hand!   60
MEPHISTOPHELES: The power inside it you now
                              understand.
The key will know the right path from the others:
follow it down – it leads you to the Mothers.
FAUST: (*With a shudder.*)
The Mothers! Why do I feel the thrill of fear?
What is that word I do not wish to hear?
MEPHISTOPHELES: So narrow-minded? Scared by a
                              new word?
Or will you only hear what you've already heard?
You're too long used to miracles to fear,
however strange the things sound you may hear.
FAUST: Nothing of good is gained by standing still.   70
Knowledge of Fear's what gives Man's Spirit wings.
The world does not allow this feeling cheaply,
but once felt, the unknown vastness moves us deeply.
MEPHISTOPHELES: Descend – or should I say ascend?
                              – it will
be all the same – fly from created things
into the boundless realm of the Ideal.
Delight in things that have long ceased to be.
The train of them will pass like clouds, unreal;
but hold them off from you. Now, use the key!
FAUST: (*Inspired.*)
Good! Firmly gripping it, my hands, my heart   80
feel new strength suddenly. Our work can start!
MEPHISTOPHELES: A burning tripod shows you, you
                            have found
your way to the deepest depths beneath the ground:
and by its light you will discern the Mothers,
some sitting, others standing up, while others

walk up and down – Formation, Transformation,
Eternal Mind's eternal re-creation.
Wreathed round with phantom forms of all creation,
they see things only in imagination;
you are invisible. But be brave! the danger's great: 90
go to the tripod, do not hesitate,
and touch it with the key.
(*FAUST, key in hand, assumes an attitude of command.*)
       That's right! And now,
like a faithful slave, the tripod follows you.
Calmly retrace your steps – let Fortune bear
you up. Before they've noticed, you're back here.
And, once you've brought the tripod back to light,
call up the heroic couple from the night:
the first to accomplish this intrepid feat,
but it is done: your conquest is complete.
The incense must obey the rites performed, 100
and into gods the smoke will be transformed.
FAUST: What now?
MEPHISTOPHELES: Bear down with your whole being.
            Strain,

then stamp and sink, and stamp and rise again.
(*FAUST stamps on the ground and vanishes into it.*)
I wonder if I should have let him go.
Will he get back? That's what I'd like to know.

5: Brightly lit hall

EMPEROR and GRANDEES. A milling crowd of COURTIERS.

CHAMBERLAIN: (*To MEPHISTOPHELES.*)
His Majesty is impatient for the show
you promised him.
CHANCELLOR: And it would not be very
wise to delay more than is necessary.
MEPHISTOPHELES: My colleague has the project well in
               hand.

The early stages have all gone as planned,
and now he's working, in complete seclusion,

to bring things to a real, sure-fire conclusion.
You see, in raising treasure of this sort,
unlike the gold, magicians must resort
to arts of utmost difficulty.

GENERAL: How   10
your friend elects to do it, is all one.

TREASURER: The Emperor just wants to see it done.
And, furthermore, he wants to see it now!

MEPHISTOPHELES: Are things as bad as that? Oh,
                              Mothers, let Faust go!

BLONDE: (*To MEPHISTOPHELES.*)
Listen! You see I have a pretty face,
but, come the summer, it is a disgrace!
My milky skin is covered up with lots
of horrid freckles, brown, unsightly spots.
Give me a cure!

MEPHISTOPHELES: You're right: it is unfair
to look like a Dalmatian half the year.   20
Take toad's tongues, mixed with frog-spawn, and distil
it very carefully when the moon is full:
when the moon wanes, then smear it smoothly on;
come Springtime, all your freckles will be gone.

BRUNETTE: The crowd all presses up to fawn on you.
I have this lame foot, and it hinders me
walking and dancing. Give me a cure too!
Even my curtseying comes off clumsily.

MEPHISTOPHELES: Let me stamp on your foot, and we
                                 shall see.

BRUNETTE: Dear me! That sounds like lovers' tit-for-tat. 30

MEPHISTOPHELES: Child, in my case, it means much
                            more than that.
Like must heal like; that is the way that we
treat all complaints now, homeopathically.
Well, then! Watch out now! And don't kick me back.
(*He stamps on her foot.*)

BRUNETTE: (*Screaming.*)
Oh! Oh! It burns! That was a vicious crack.
Just like a mule.

MEPHISTOPHELES: The cure lies in attack.
    Now you can dance as long as you are able,
    and squeeze your lover's foot, under the table.
LADY: (*Pressing forward.*)
    Let me through there! I can no more disguise
    the pains that plunge my heart in misery.   40
    He, who till yesterday, lived only in my eyes,
    now just has eyes for her, and turns his back on me.
MEPHISTOPHELES: Here, take this coal, sneak up to
                          him, and brush
    his sleeve or coat with it. He'll feel a rush
    of true remorse. Then swallow the coal at once,
    and don't drink anything. The amorous dunce
    will sigh for your embraces before nightfall.
LADY: It isn't poison?
MEPHISTOPHELES: Give my art its rightful
    measure of due attention and respect.
    To find a coal like this, you'd need to make   50
    a long, long journey. It comes from a stake,
    the sort we used to burn to some effect.
PAGE: I'm in love: but they say I'm just a boy.
MEPHISTOPHELES. (*Aside.*)
    You'd think that they were doing it to annoy.
    (*To the PAGE.*)
    Don't chase the young ones: the maturer crew
    will know exactly what to do with you.
    (*Others come crowding up to him.*)
    And still they come! Fighting, red in tooth
    and claw. I'll have to fall back on the truth.
    Never a good idea! But needs must when
    the Devil drives. Mothers! Let Faust return again!   60
    Or I'll reluctantly be forced to practise
    improvisatory delaying tactics.
    The play begins! The Emperor commands –
    the curtain draws aside – the space expands
    into a...theatre! Arcane, exciting,
    bathing us all in dim, mysterious lighting.
ASTROLOGER: A mighty temple of the ancient days
    rises, by magic, to our astonished gaze.

ARCHITECT: Now is that classical? It won't do at all.
　　Crude, coarse and clumsy, that's what I should call　　70
　　it; people really have such odd criteria,
　　saying such things are good. They can't be serious.
　　I must admit, my tastes are more particular.
　　Give me the cool good sense of Perpendicular.
　　Sometimes my soul feels literally parched
　　for the simplicity of the Gothic arch;
　　at other moments, goodness, how one craves
　　the sturdy common-sense of Norman naves.
　　Do buildings such as *this* give the soul wings to fly?
　　No, such an edifice can never edify.　　80
　　(*FAUST rises on the other side of the proscenium arch.*)
FAUST: (*Majestically.*)
　　Oh, Mothers, in your name, each on your throne,
　　in boundless space, eternally alone,
　　and yet at one; about your heads are weaving
　　images of Life, moving, and yet not living.
　　In multifarious visions, all the past
　　moves there: what has once been is never lost.
　　This you dispense, beings of matchless might,
　　under the roof of day, the bowl of night.
　　Some are caught up in Life's magnetic course,
　　others called up by magic charms of force:　　90
　　prodigal, fearless, the magician brings
　　the longed-for visions of miraculous things.
ASTROLOGER: The glowing key has barely touched the bowl,
　　than vaporous mists begin to cover all.
　　Moving, they float in music without cease;
　　now recognise a spirit-masterpiece.
FAUST: Empty your minds of thought, to give a free
　　unfettered rein to fantasy.
　　The image you desired and now perceive
　　cannot exist, yet, seeing, we believe.　　100
ASTROLOGER: Obedient to the Magus, now there rises
　　the miracle before our very eyes. Is
　　there one of you can doubt this lovely boy
　　is unmistakably Paris, Prince of Troy?

COURTIERS/LADIES: (*Variously.*)

Oh, the glow of strength, the bloom of youth!

Fresh as a peach, and twice as juicy!

                                              Truth!

Such a well-chiselled and voluptuous lip.

A cup where you might like to take a sip?

Pretty, but not quite our class, don't you know?
He could be just a touch more *comme-il-faut*.   110

I'm bound to say, it *is* a pretty face;
but don't you find it rather commonplace?

He certainly could use a bit more grace.

He seems to me a common shepherd-lad,
unpolished, coarse, and, frankly, underbred.

Half-naked boys have great charm, often as not:
put 'em in armour, though – soon see what's what.

Look how he sits! The languorous grace of it!

Is his lap somewhere you might like to sit?

Stretching his arms so prettily over his head...   120

No, really, that should be prohibited!

You men – why must you always criticise?

Lolling, before the Emperor's very eyes!
It isn't done! Look at him, stretching and scratching!

I only hope he's not got something catching.

It's acting. He's supposed to be alone.

Art has a duty to respect the throne!

Oh, look, he's gone to sleep. How very sweet!

A few good snores – the illusion is complete.
(*HELEN appears.*)

MEPHISTOPHELES: And here she is. I'd lose no sleep
                                    for her.   130

Pretty, but not the sort that I prefer.

FAUST: Have I still eyes? The spring of loveliness
    wells prodigally up and floods my soul.
    My dreadful journey now was all worthwhile.
    The world was closed to me: how could I guess
    what, since my priesthood, it would come to be?
    Miraculous, established, permanency!
    Let life and breath and all be torn from me,
    if ever this, my new-found faith, should lapse.
    The magic mirror once deceived my mind   140
    with a false vision of beauty. Redefined
    in the light of your loveliness, mirages collapse.
    To you I owe the concept of all passion,
    strength, adoration, worship, dedication,
    love, madness, intermittence of the heart.
MEPHISTOPHELES: (*From the prompter's box.*)
    Control yourself! That isn't in your part.
COURTIERS/LADIES: (*Variously.*)
    The figure's well enough, but the head's too small.

    Look at her feet! No, she won't do at all.

    Quite, quite lovely! My experienced guess is
    she's probably one of those foreign princesses.   150

    She leans towards him, softly, stealthily…

    How plain, next to his youthful purity!

    Her beauty gives a sheen to all it shines upon.

    A work of art – the Moon sleeps with Endymion!

    Exactly! Now the goddess seems to sink,
    bending as if his breath were meat and drink.

    A kiss!

        His cup runs over!

            Enviable!

    And all of this in public! It's intolerable!
FAUST: No. No. She mustn't kiss him!
MEPHISTOPHELES: Quiet! Be still!
    They're phantoms: leave them to do what they will.   160

COURTIERS/LADLES: (*Variously.*)
    And now she turns to him with easy grace.
    She feels the need to take the boy in hand.

    Why men should always think, in such a case,
    that they're the first, I'll never understand.

    She steals away – he wakes, as from a trance.

    Just as I thought – she takes a backward glance.

    He is aroused – new feelings in him stir.

    I don't suppose they're very new to her.

    The wonder of it brings him to his knees.

    She hardly shows surprise at what she sees. 170

    Gad! There's a woman after my own heart.

    If you ask me, a vulgar little tart.

    I'd like to be in his shoes for a start.

    Who wouldn't be a fish in such a net?

    She's been through quite a few hands, don't forget.

    The glitter must have rubbed off quite a bit.

    At ten, she was already doing it.

    These days, a man must often eat up what he's given.

    A plate of scraps like that? I'd be in seventh Heaven!
PROFESSOR: I must confess, that, though I plainly see 180
    her, we've no proof of her identity.
    Knowing how actual experience can lead
    one into error, I trust only what I read.
    The *Iliad* tells us that the real Helen
    aroused the Trojan greybeards past all telling.
    They all agreed the ten years' war had been
    well worth it for the rape of such a queen.
    Now, she fits that description to perfection:
    though I'm not young, I feel a big…attraction.
    I'm sure I do beg everybody's pardon, 190
    I only meant that she gives me a…
ASTROLOGER: Hard on
    the heels of boyhood strides the hero; his

two arms enfold her. She can scarce resist.
With young, strong, grasp he lifts her in the air.
Will he abduct her?

FAUST: No, you fool! Take care!
You'll ruin everything! Are you deaf? Stay!

MEPHISTOPHELES: Remember just who's putting on this
play!

PROFESSOR: One word more – all that remains to tell in
this drama should be called *The Rape of Helen*.

FAUST: Rape? Do I count for nothing here? Was it for this   200
that I came back from all the horrors of the waste
of storm and surge that formed that dreadful emptiness?
And now my feet rest on sure ground at last:
I stand my ground, then. Reality is here,
where my spirit may vie with other spirits, where
the mighty double spirit-world may be prepared.
Though she is far away, how could she be
nearer? I'll save her – she'll belong to me
twice over! Mothers! Mothers! Let it be so.
The man who once has had her cannot let her go.   210

ASTROLOGER: What are you doing? Faustus! Violently
he seizes her – the figure fades away;
and now towards the boy he turns the key,
touches him – horror!

MEPHISTOPHELES: You cannot change the past. A
single interference means disaster.
This is complete calamity. Oh, no!
(*A terrific explosion. FAUST lies stretched out on the ground.
The spirits vanish in mist.*)
(*Hoisting FAUST over his shoulder.*)
Well, there you have it. Even the Devil, once he's taken
on a fool, must look alive to save his bacon.
Devils and fools will never mix with ease.
He who lies down with dogs, gets up with fleas.   220

End of Act One.

ACT TWO

1: A high-vaulted, narrow Gothic chamber, formerly Faust's, unchanged

MEPHISTOPHELES steps out from behind a curtain. As he lifts it and looks back, we see FAUST stretched out on an antiquated bed.

MEPHISTOPHELES: Lie there, then, luckless, witless
                                             victim of
the invisible, unbreakable chain of Love!
The man whom Helena decides to seize on
may take some time recovering his reason.
(*Looking about him.*)
Just as it was the day I came!
The paper's yellow, the ink has dried,
the spiders' webs have multiplied,
but otherwise it's just the same.
Even the pen's still here, with which he signed
his soul away to the Enemy of Mankind.   10
Look! on the nib, there actually is still
a drop of the blood that I coaxed him to spill.
Such a collector's piece must touch the heart
of every amateur of works of art.
(*To the juvenile section of the audience, which is not applauding.*)
I see my words have left you cold.
Dear children! I shan't take offence.
Remember that the Devil's old:
grow up! you'll find that he makes sense.

2: Laboratory in the Mediaeval style

Clumsy and elaborate equipment for bizarre uses.

WAGNER: (*At the furnace.*)
The dreadful bell rings out, its tongue
sets these sooty walls vibrating.
Uncertainty must not prolong

this fearful period of waiting.
The darkness clears, and in the phial,
glowing like a living coal,
now, like a precious jewel, a spark
flashes like lightning through the dark;
at last I see a bright, white light ascend –
Oh, do not let me lose it, as before... 10
Oh, God! who's rattling at the door?

MEPHISTOPHELES: (*Entering.*)
May I come in? I enter as a friend.

WAGNER: (*In some agitation.*)
Bid welcome to the hour of destiny.
Just hold your breath and look on silently.
A mighty work's conclusion's what you're seeing?

MEPHISTOPHELES: Namely?

WAGNER: The creation of a human being.

MEPHISTOPHELES: What? Do you mean you've got a
loving couple
making a good old-fashioned two-backed beast?

WAGNER: Dear God, no! That old-fashioned way's the least
efficient and a great deal too much trouble. 20
That sort of thing's all very well for brutes.
Mankind needs something nobler, that suits
his nobler nature. Yes! The deed of kind,
in future, must be totally redesigned.
(*He turns back to the furnace.*)
It's glowing! – look, it's getting clear –
the consummation's nearly there.
It's working! What you see is Science's solution
of Nature's greatest mystery – Evolution.
What she took so long to organise,
we've understood, and so can crystallise. 30

MEPHISTOPHELES: The longer you live the more you see.
Nothing in this world surprises me.
The list of things that I've already seen,
surely includes a crystallised human being.

WAGNER: Listen! It's moving! What more could I ask?
The cloudiness disperses to unmask

my little creature to the light of day.
The ringing becomes speech – what will it say?
HOMUNCULUS: (*Speaking to WAGNER out of the phial.*)
Pppaaapppaaa – Well, how are you? That was close!
Embrace me! Not too tight! Don't break the glass!   40
That is the property of matter – all
of space can hardly hold the natural
creation, but Man's work must be restrained
within a framework, where it is contained.
That is the limitation of Man's art.
(*To MEPHISTOPHELES.*)
My good-for-nothing cousin, you here too?
Good timing! While I live, I must have things to do.
Give me an indication where to start.
WAGNER: Just one word first. Tell me, how can the soul
and body so be fused in a perfect whole,   50
yet be at constant loggerheads all their lives?
MEPHISTOPHELES: Ask rather why men quarrel with
their wives.
A question to which you'll never find an answer.
Our little friend wants work to do. Come on, Sir!
HOMUNCULUS: Where do we go?
MEPHISTOPHELES: (*Pointing to a side-door.*)
There's something to employ
your gifts on.
WAGNER: (*Still gazing at the phial.*)
I have made a really pretty boy.
(*The side-door opens; FAUST is seen stretched out on a couch.*)
HOMUNCULUS: (*Astonished.*)
Significant!
(*The phial slips out of WAGNER's hands, and hovers above
FAUST, shedding light over him.*)
Is it reality, or a dream
surrounds him? In a grove, a crystal stream,
by which the fairest forest nymphs undress,
one of them, of surpassing loveliness,   60
stands out from all the rest. What sudden noise
of beating wings, what splashing now destroys

the water-mirror? All the nymphs have fled:
all but the Queen, who sees, with quiet pride,
the amorous Swan-prince pressing to her side,
tamed but persistent, thrusting in her lap...
but suddenly I see a cloud arise,
to shroud the beauty of it from our eyes.

MEPHISTOPHELES: So much imagination for such a
little chap.
I can't see anything.

HOMUNCULUS: Of course. Brought forth   70
in the dark ages of the Gothic North,
reared in a muddle of knight-errantry,
mixed in with crude religious bigotry,
is it surprising you've no eyes to see?
Where you belong is in obscurity.
These murky grey surroundings are
too dismal for our dreamer there by far.
If he wakes up in here, we shall have got
new worries – he'll drop dead upon the spot.
Dreaming of swans and nymphs, he cannot wake   80
to such a scene – the shock would be too great.
I'm easy-going, but I really hate
this sort of place. Let's get him out of here.

MEPHISTOPHELES: I like the plan. Let's go at once. But
where?

HOMUNCULUS: We'll take our journey back to the Antique:
something cool and classical – and Greek.

MEPHISTOPHELES: Why there, if I'm allowed to put the
question?
Those Attic heroes give me indigestion.

HOMUNCULUS: You only think romantic ghosts believable:
your genuine ghost is also classical.   90

MEPHISTOPHELES: Their epic struggles bore me: soon
as one
is finished, then another has begun.
They say they're fighting to preserve Democracy,
but it's just slave against slave, as far as I can see.

HOMUNCULUS: Mens' nature is to brawl; leave them alone.
Each must defend himself as best he can

from boyhood – that's how he becomes a man.
Our problem is – how do we cure this one?
MEPHISTOPHELES: I've several cures, but all of them
                                        Romantic:
   but you seem quite determined on the Antique.   100
   I've never thought those Greeks were up to much;
   all that free-living sensuality, and such,
   is quite attractive, but, for Sense of Sin,
   compared to us, they simply don't begin.
   What next?
HOMUNCULUS: Wrap the cloak about
   the pair of you. It should bear you all right.
   I'll light the way.
WAGNER: What about me?
HOMUNCULUS: Ah, you
   will stay at home, you have a lot to do.
   Important work: unroll your scrolls, and try
   to find, in all those books, the Reason Why;   110
   reflect upon the What; sit pondering
   the How of things while we go wandering,
   you *may* unveil the dot upon the 'I'.
   Goodbye!
WAGNER: Goodbye? But it would break my heart
   to think a time had come for us to part.
MEPHISTOPHELES: On to Peneios! We must make a start.
   (*To the audience.*)
   When you come down to it, I am afraid
   we all depend on creatures we have made.

3: Classical Walpurgis Night – the Pharsalian fields

Darkness. Travellers in the air, above.

HOMUNCULUS: Once more circle overhead –
   ghostly scenes of fire and dread
   spread themselves before our eyes.
MEPHISTOPHELES: Horrid ghosts stalk through the gloom –
   here I can feel quite at home
   with something I can recognise.

HOMUNCULUS: Set him down here close at hand –
   to find his new life in this land
   of myth and legend where he lies.
FAUST: (*As he touches ground.*)
   Where is she? No more questions now, among   10
   such scenes – if this is not the grass that bore
   her footprint, nor the wave that broke before
   her, it is still the air that speaks her tongue.
   Now I, the sleeper, like Antaeus, fired
   with energy afresh, rise up inspired
   to seek her, come what may, through all this maze
   of tortuous and labyrinthine ways.
   (*He withdraws.*)

4: The slopes of the Upper Peneios

MEPHISTOPHELES: (*Prying around.*)
   Wandering round this fiery field, I've been
   disgusted and repelled by what I've seen.
   Most of them naked, the odd shirt at most,
   sphinxes, giant ants, gryphons, a shameless host
   of all manner of creatures, winged and hairy,
   offering back and front views to the unwary.
   Although, like all the rest of you, I find
   perpetual solace in a dirty mind,
   I cannot stomach the lack of ambiguity
   with which these things were treated in antiquity.   10
   Today we like such things, however quaint,
   to be treated with some style and more restraint.
   Disgusting things! Still – I'm a guest – they're due
   good manners. May I introduce myself?
SPHINX: And who are you?
MEPHISTOPHELES: I go by many names. Perhaps there are
   some English people here? They travel far
   to visit battlefields and classic sites,
   ruins, and similar tourists' delights.
   (This place should suit them right down to the ground.)
   In their more primitive drama I am found   20
   as Old Iniquity, or Nick for short.

SPHINX: What is the point of that?

MEPHISTOPHELES: I've never thought.

SPHINXES: Perhaps – Perhaps not – I don't like his face –
    Why is he here? – He just looks out of place.

MEPHISTOPHELES: You think your visitor would hesitate
    to match his claws against your own? Just wait.

SPHINXES: If you insist – However long you dwell
    among us, you will finally expel
    yourself – At home, you may do as you please,
    but here you really feel quite ill-at-ease.   30

MEPHISTOPHELES: Your top halves make a really
                                 pretty show;
    what worries me more is the beast below.

SPHINXES: Kettle! Just listen to the pot.
    Our claws are sound, your hoof is not.
    (*SIRENS preluding up above.*)

MEPHISTOPHELES: What are those birds that sing up there?

SPHINXES: Sirens. They'll be your doom, beware!

SIRENS: Ah, why seek to cloy your heart
    with that odious, monstrous crew?
    Listen, as we flock to you,
    voices tuned in every part,   40
    as befits the Sirens' art.

SPHINXES: (*Mocking them to the same tune.*)
    Force them to come down. As long
    as in the trees they hide their strong
    and dreadful claws, like birds of prey,
    they will maul you, if you stay
    and listen to the Sirens' song.

SIRENS: Hate and envy, both begone!
    All joy is gathered in our song
    that exists beneath the sky.
    Now be seen on land and sea,   50
    every sign of amity
    man can greet his fellow by.

MEPHISTOPHELES: Music's thrown away on me.
    Ear-catching, granted, it may be,
    but my heart it cannot touch.

SPHINXES: Heart? – How can you speak of such
    a thing? – A leather bag in place
    of one would suit your ugly face.
FAUST: (*Entering.*)
    How wonderful! The sight of them contents me:
    repulsive, yes, but strong, and somehow great.   60
    I sense already an auspicious fate.
    That serious look of theirs – where will it send me?
    (*Referring to the SPHINXES.*)
    In front of such as these, stood Oedipus.
    (*Referring to the SIRENS.*)
    In ropes before those, writhed Odysseus.
    (*To the SPHINXES.*)
    Woman-faced sphinxes – answer me, you who dwell in
    the shadow of the pyramids – who has seen Helen?
SPHINX: We were extinct, long before she was born –
    The last of us was killed by Heracles –
    Go to consult the centaur, Chiron, he's
    the only one from whom you'll ever learn.   70

5: On the Lower Peneios

SPHINXES: At the pyramid's broad base,
    we sit in judgment on the nations:
    war and peace and inundations
    we see with unchanging face.

    Sister, sisters, can you hear?
    What is that insistent sound?
    Louder, clearer, coming near,
    hoofbeats drumming on the ground.
FAUST: It is the centaur! Chiron, halt! And let me speak
    with you.
CHIRON: I may not. Mount! Now tell me what you seek.   10
FAUST: You taught and formed, with wisdom, strength and
                           grace,
    the greatest heroes of a hero-race.
    In their noblest footsteps you have trod,
    and lived the hard life of a demigod.
    Whom did you think the greatest of all these?

CHIRON: Do not awaken tender memories...
　　When first I saw the youthful Heracles,
　　I knew why men worship divinities.
　　So beautiful, and born to be a king, although
　　loyal to his elder brother, and to women too.　　　20
　　His equal never will be seen again on Earth,
　　nor Art ever convey a fraction of his worth.
FAUST: Art is of no use at such times, as I know.
　　But tell me about the loveliest woman now.
CHIRON: What? Women's beauty? Just an empty phrase –
　　too often a frozen picture, arid, dead.
　　The only ones that I can truly praise
　　are those in whom Life overflows, who are glad
　　to be alive. Beauty may be pleased
　　with simply being beautiful, but she's　　　30
　　dependent upon grace to overpower
　　us, grace such as Helen had, whom I once bore
　　on my back.
FAUST:　　　You carried her?
CHIRON:　　　　　　　　As I now do you.
FAUST: As if I was not dazed enough before...
　　To know that I am sitting where she sat!
CHIRON: Grasping the same hair that you're tugging at!
　　Stroking my dripping flanks, so sweet, so self-possessed,
　　so winning, and so young – an old man's happiness.
FAUST: But she was only ten!
CHIRON:　　　　　　　I see the academics
　　have hoaxed you, like themselves, with their polemics.　　　40
　　The heroine of mythology is free
　　from Time – the artist thinks of her as he
　　wishes to see her, neither young nor old,
　　and always looking good enough to eat;
　　ravished in childhood, still courted when she's old.
　　Enough! The Poet Time cannot defeat.
FAUST: Nor shall it conquer her. How rare, how great a chance
　　to snatch one's love from the clutch of circumstance!
　　You saw her once, as I saw her today, and if
　　I cannot live with her, I would not wish to live.　　　50

CHIRON: Strange creature! Caught in the raptures of your
                                                        kind –
  to immortals you appear to have lost your mind.
  But we meet opportunely, nonetheless,
  since, for a moment, on this night, each year,
  I visit Manto, the great prophetess.
  She will be able to effect your cure.
FAUST: I want no cure. Love has made me too proud
  to be dragged down to the level of the crowd.
CHIRON: Never, never name the fountain
  out of which you will not drink.   60
  This is the place. Begin to think,
  and quickly too, about dismounting.
MANTO: (*Dreaming.*)
  Hoofbeats shake the air,
  vibrate the sacred stair;
  demigods are near.
CHIRON: Quite right. Open your eyes – I'm here.
MANTO: (*Waking.*)
  Welcome! You never miss a year.
CHIRON: Not while you're still in practice here.
MANTO: Still the same wandering restlessness?
CHIRON: Still the same solitary peacefulness?   70
  Through Space and Time I circle ceaselessly.
MANTO: I wait in Space – and Time revolves round me.
  And who is this?
CHIRON: The night has brought
  him here to you. He is distraught –
  his mind, though firmly set on winning
  Helen, is stuck for a beginning.
  A proper patient for your healing fires.
MANTO: I love all those who nurse impossible desires.
  (*CHIRON is already a long way off.*)
  Come down, daring young man, experience
  hope and joy, where Queen Persephone   80
  secretly grants forbidden audience:
  I smuggled Orpheus in, in days gone by.
  The warning he was given went unheeded.
  Be brave now! Put your chance to better use than he did.
  (*They descend.*)

6: Back on the Upper Peneios

SIRENS: Plunge into Peneios' stream!
    Swimming, revel and rejoice,
    raise, in song on song, the voice
    of which unhappy nations dream.
    Without water, none is spared:
    let us seek the Aegean Sea,
    leading our bright company
    to where all pleasures shall be shared.
    (*Earthquake.*)
MEPHISTOPHELES: (*On the plain.*)
    Though I know how to manage Northern witches,
    I'm none too happy with these foreign bitches.   10
    At home, though things mayn't look as nice as this,
    at least one knows exactly where one is.
    But here! At any moment, how d'you know
    the ground won't suddenly rear up, from below,
    a mountain – maybe not what the Swiss would call
    a mountain – nevertheless quite tall
    enough to block the Sphinxes from my view.
    (*Enter the LAMIAE.*)
    What's this attractive, if disorderly, crew?
    The curse of Man since Adam's time still lies
    on us. We all grow old – but who grows wise?   20
    The hallmark of the human race is
    tight corseting and painted faces.
    All these once knew of good, they have forgot:
    touch them, their limbs well nigh fall off with rot.
    We know it in our bones, yet still we prance
    like puppets – when the carrion pipes, we dance.
LAMIAE: Stop! – He's thinking – Look, he stands:
    don't let him slip through our hands.
MEPHISTOPHELES: I shall press ahead without
    tangling in the web of Doubt;   30
    if there were no such things as witches,
    who'd be in the Devil's britches?

LAMIAE: Circle round him once or twice.
Love will soon entangle him,
forcing him to make a choice.

MEPHISTOPHELES: Thought the light is pretty dim,
you seem not unprepossessing,
nor too dear for my possessing.
Really quite attractive creatures,
with some most unusual features.   40

EMPUSA: (*Pushing forward.*)
And so have I – so let me join!

LAMIAE: Really, she is too annoying.

MEPHISTOPHELES: The one advantage of vacations,
is not encountering one's relations:
still, to quote an old cliché,
the world gets smaller every day.

EMPUSA: I know how to act decisively:
I could transform myself indefinitely.
But I've put on my ass's head: it
is in your honour, to do you credit.   50

MEPHISTOPHELES: I notice that these Southern people feel
family ties should count for a great deal:
nevertheless, I would not wish it said
I was related to an ass's head.

LAMIAE: Why all the hesitation? – Don't look back –
I bet he's a disaster in the sack.

MEPHISTOPHELES: I'll have the little one over yonder!
(*Embracing her.*)
Damn! Changed into a six-foot anaconda!
Well, then, the big tall one might do all right.
(*Seizing another.*)
Changed to a broomstick! This is not my night.   60
There is the plump one: yes, I see
a genuine possibility.
Soft, firm and chubby – just the sort of piece
to fetch high prices in the Middle East.
Third time lucky. Let me at her!
(*Grabs her.*)
Devil take it! An empty bladder!

LAMIAE: Leave the offensive witches' son
    on his own – The fool has come
    off cheap, when all is said and done.
    (*They go.*)
MEPHISTOPHELES: Much wiser I am not, that much is
                             clear; 70
    the North's absurd, but no more so than here.
    Where am I going now? Where am I, then?
    Where are my Sphinxes to be found again?
    What is that light that fades and glows?
    It's gone. No, there it is! It comes and goes.
    The way that things work out, well nigh miraculous:
    my little artificial friend – Homunculus!
    where have you been?
HOMUNCULUS: Floating around impatiently,
    longing to smash my glass and be
    a real being, though from what   80
    I've seen of the world so far, I'm not
    so sure I really want to start.
    I have discovered two philosophers,
    who talk incessantly of 'Nature'; one
    claims life is water, while the other avers
    the source of all created energy's the sun.
    But doubtless from them I shall soon find out
    the best and safest way to bring my birth about.
MEPHISTOPHELES: To be reborn? Then do it on your own.
    Without mistakes, nothing is truly known.   90
HOMUNCULUS: Still, good advice is not a thing to flout.
MEPHISTOPHELES: Off with you, then. We'll see how
                         things turn out.
    (*They separate. The two philosophers enter.*)
ANAXAGORAS: Will nothing penetrate your stubborn mind?
    Or are you quite impervious to the truth?
THALES: The wave will yield to any wind,
    yet from the rock it keeps aloof.
ANAXAGORAS: Fiery vapour brought this rock to birth.
THALES: Moisture made all organic life on earth.
HOMUNCULUS: Allow me to take notes on this:
    I hunger after genesis.   100

ANAXAGORAS: Have you ever seen a cliff of such a height,
    made from wet mud, and in a single night?
THALES: Nature does not exert her fluid powers
    according to a man-made scheme of days and hours.
    She shapes things by her own decree, and hence
    even in the Grand Design, there is no violence.
ANAXAGORAS: Yes, there *was* here. The volcano burst the
                                      earth,
    bringing the mountain to immediate birth.
THALES: This argument won't get us anywhere.
    The mountain undeniably is there.   110
    (*To HOMUNCULUS.*)
    Now to your little problem. We shall visit
    Proteus, the god of Metamorphosis. It
    will be the best advice you'll get, since he
    specialises in Mutability.
    (*They withdraw. MEPHISTOPHELES clambers up on the
    other side.*)
MEPHISTOPHELES: Over these rocky crags, and knotted
                              roots of oak,
    I pick my way, and find it uphill work.
    On my beloved Harz at home, the pines give off
    the scent of pitch, which I most dearly love,
    well...next to brimstone – but down here in Greece,
    of smells like that, I haven't found a trace.   120
    What I should really like to know, is what
    they use to keep Hell's fires and torments hot?
DRYAD: Why limit your thoughts to those of your own land?
    Worship the sacred oak-trees near at hand.
MEPHISTOPHELES: We always recall the things we sacrifice;
    what we've been used to, that is Paradise.
    But what's that crouching thing that I can see
    in the dim light of that cave? Or are there three?
DRYAD: The Phorkyads! Approach them undismayed,
    and talk to them – if you are not afraid.   130
MEPHISTOPHELES: Why not? Let's look at them. I am
                              amazed!
    Proud as I am, I must confess
    I never saw the like in all my days;

they're worse than mandrake-roots for ugliness.
We would not let such foul abortions dwell
on the back doorstep of our foulest Hell!
They stir: they seem to sense that I am here.
Their bat-like vampire squeaking fills the air.
PHORKYADS: Sisters, let me have the eye, to see
    who approaches our temple so audaciously.   140
MEPHISTOPHELES: Ladies, your most obedient! Have
                        I leave
to enter, your triple blessing to receive?
Though I appear a stranger at your gate, it
seems fair to say we're distantly related.
The ancient gods I've seen and still revere;
I've bowed the knee before both Ops and Rhea;
the Parcae, kin to Chaos and to you,
I saw last night – or was it two nights ago? –
but the like of you I never saw before.
I'm speechless, thunderstruck – need I say more?   150
PHORKYADS: This spirit seems not unintelligent.
MEPHISTOPHELES: That no poet has sung your fame
                       surprises me.
No pictures, sculptures? How can such things be?
And how can artists be so negligent?
PHORKYADS: None of us three have let such thoughts
                         intrude
upon our darkness and our solitude.
MEPHISTOPHELES: Indeed, how should you, living in
                      this grot,
the world forgetting, by the world forgot?
You should be living in those splendid regions
where Art and Grandeur claim a like allegiance.   160
Where each new day, agilely, at the double,
a living hero steps forth from the marble!
Where...
PHORKYADS: Stop! Don't tempt us to learn any more:
what gain is that on what we knew before?
Night-born ourselves, night-creatures our only brothers,
scarce knowing ourselves, and quite unknown to others.

MEPHISTOPHELES: In such a case there's not a lot to say,
    but we can transform ourselves another way.
    One eye, one tooth suffices for all three,
    but it would still fit, mythologically,   170
    if you'd subsume the essence of all three
    in two, and leave the other one to me.
    Just for a while?
FIRST PHORKYAD: How say you? Should we try?
SECOND PHORKYAD: We'll risk it – but without the
                                  tooth or eye.
MEPHISTOPHELES: But surely, if you take away the best,
    the lack of it invalidates the rest.
THIRD PHORKYAD: Screw up an eye, that's easy done;
    stick out a canine tooth, just one.
    And, from the side, you'll surely be
    the sisterly image of we three.   180
MEPHISTOPHELES: I'm honoured. So be it.
PHORKYADS: Agreed then!
MEPHISTOPHELES: (*Standing in profile, as a PHORKYAD.*)
                                     There!
    Chaos's well-beloved son stands here!
PHORKYADS: We arc her *daughters*, by immemorial right.
MEPHISTOPHELES: Shame! must I be called
                            hermaphrodite?
PHORKYADS: Look at us, sisters! Your new beauties prize:
    our triad has two teeth now, and two eyes!
MEPHISTOPHELES: I shall withdraw from *all* eyes for a
                                spell,
    then scare the devils in the pit of Hell.

7: Rocky inlets of the Aegean Sea

The moon pauses at its zenith. SIRENS lie on the cliffs, fluting and singing to the moon.

SIRENS: If, in dark Thessalian night,
    witches, with their hideous rite,
    drew you down, with blasphemy,
    watch, from the tranquillity
    of your night, the trembling sea.

Light the glowing throng that rides
on the phosphorescent tides,
and illumine, with your quiet
light, the ocean's seething riot.
We, your servants, one and all,   10
beg you, Moon, be merciful!
THALES: Proteus, where are you?
PROTEUS: (*Ventriloquising, now near, now distant.*)
                    Here!
            Here!
                        Here!
        Here!
                            Here!
ANAXAGORAS: Very amusing – could you not appear
to please an old friend, and stop being clever?
THALES: We've seen these tricks before.
PROTEUS: (*As if from a distance.*)
                          Farewell for ever.
Farewell.
ANAXAGORAS: (*To HOMUNCULUS.*)
            He's near. Now shine out, bright.
He's nosy as a fish. The light
will bring him here to us. He will be stopped
by it, whatever form he may adopt.   20
HOMUNCULUS: I'll do my best, but I must take
some care, or else the glass may break.
PROTEUS: (*Appearing in the form of a gigantic turtle.*)
What is that shines so prettily? What is it?
THALES: Come nearer then, if you don't want to miss it.
And, if it's not too much bother, for the form,
please come in some shape closer to the norm:
it is our privilege to decide if we
agree to show you what you want to see.
PROTEUS: Come now! That is the oldest trick on earth.
THALES: Changing shape still seems to cause you mirth.   30
    (*He reveals HOMUNCULUS.*)
PROTEUS: A luminous midget! First I've ever seen!
THALES: He needs advice, to be a human being.
The way he told it us, he came to earth

only half-formed, a sort of virgin birth;
not short of qualities of the Ideal,
but up to now, he's lacking in the Real.
Till now, only the glass has given him weight;
but now he longs to achieve a corporal state.

PROTEUS: A virgin's son, as genuine as he could be,
being there much sooner than he should be! 40

THALES: (*Quietly.*)

There is another point that's somewhat critical;
I think the little chap's hermaphroditical.

PROTEUS: So much the better – when he arrives,
he can lead the best of all possible lives.
But now we need have no hesitation.
Life must begin, for him, in the Ocean;
first, as a micro-organism, then
proceeding through the stage of valve and fin,
developing naturally, by evolution,
into the higher forms of animal creation. 50

Life on earth must always be
merest toil and drudgery:
in water, life is lived with ease;
come to those eternal seas
with Dolphin-Proteus.
(*He transforms himself into a dolphin.*)
                          I am he!
Riding on me, you shall lack
for nothing – mounted on my back,
I shall wed you to the sea!

THALES: Take up the generous invitation –
a helter-skelter through Creation's 60
evolutionary plan.
Ascend, by laws fixed by the ages,
evolving through a million stages,
to reach, at last, the state of Man.
(*HOMUNCULUS mounts the dolphin PROTEUS.*)

SIRENS: Softly gliding, gently sliding,
ring on ring, and line on line,
round the chariot come riding,

sinuous and serpentine!
Nereids, approach, draw near,
in savage strength and loveliness,   70
bring with you sweet Galatea,
image of her mother's grace;
solemn, god-like gravity,
worthy immortality,
radiant beauty, of more worth
than all the daughters of the earth!
(*GALATEA approaches, riding on a sea-shell.*)
NEREUS: My best-loved Galatea, here at last!
GALATEA: Oh, father! Such rapture! My gaze is held fast
by so much beauty. Oh, my dolphins, stay!
NEREUS: They are gone already, moving away   80
in widening circles, they depart,
careless of the turmoil of the heart.
If they would take me with them, over there...
but a single glimpse repays an empty year.
THALES. Hail, Galatea! We worship you!
My spirit flowers again, thrust through
by knowledge of the beautiful, the true!

Ocean, vital element,
all Creation's nourishment,
reign over us through all eternity.   90
HOMUNCULUS: In this fluid element,
what my light illuminates,
is wonderful, miraculous to see.
PROTEUS: This life-giving element
gives your light embellishment,
and weds it to the music of the sea.
NEREUS: What mystery now sets itself in motion
among the multitudinous hosts of Ocean?
What flames round the feet of my child, round her shell?
Now powerful, now gentle, it seems now to swell   100
and pulse as if the light were moved by Love.
THALES: Proteus has seduced Homunculus...
these are the unmistakable symptoms of
desire overmastering – the glass

will shatter at his touch: he'll be destroyed.
It shudders – his essence is poured into the Void.
SIRENS: What marvel transfigures the waters? They smite
    against one another in glory. The night
    reveals all forms of Life in a wonder of Fire.
    Praise Eros, in whom all things live and expire!   110

    Praise the ocean! Praise the surge
    on which the sacred fires converge!
    Praise the water! Praise the fire!
    Praise the rare adventure's power!
TUTTI: Praise the gentle wind's soft breath!
    Praise the secret caves of earth!
    Praise and honour evermore
    to the elements, all four.

    Praise the water! Praise the fire!
    Praise the earth! And praise the air!   120
    Praised be all four elements,
    reigning in omnipotence!

End of Act Two.

ACT THREE

1: In front of the Palace of Menelaus at Sparta

HELEN of Troy enters with a CHORUS of captive Trojan women,
led by PANTHALIS.

HELEN: I, Helen, much admired, and much abused, have come
    from yonder shore, where lately we have disembarked,
    still giddy from the rocking surge of restless seas.
    Down on the shore, surrounded by his bravest men,
    King Menelaus celebrates his safe return.
    Great house! It is from you I wish my welcome home,
    through whose great doors once Menelaus strode,
    chosen from many suitors, come to marry me.
    And now, returned from Troy, my lord sends me ahead
    into the city, though his thought I cannot guess.   10
    For while we were in the ship, he seldom looked
    at me, nor scarcely spoke a single cheering word,
    but sat there like a man with mischief in his heart.
    But barely had the foremost ships found anchorage,
    he spoke like one inspired: 'Go! Seek the house,
    assemble all the servants whom we left behind;
    and when you have seen all things duly ordered right,
    then take such tripods as a sacrifice requires,
    and see that water from the sacred fountains is
    available, and that a store of seasoned wood   20
    is ready, which will swiftly catch the living flame.
    Nor, finally, omit the sacrificial axe.
    All else that may be fitting, I leave in your own hands.'
    He spoke, and bade me leave at once, but did not name
    what living creature he would offer to the gods.
    It is suspicious, but I cast off further care,
    referring all things to the judgment of the gods
    who bring to pass whatever they conceive in thought.
    This may be evil, or it may be good, but men
    must bear it, as a part of earthly destiny.   30
    Then come what may – whatever lies ahead – I must

go up without delay into the royal house,
my longed-for home, long-missed and nearly forfeited.
(*She pauses on the threshold of the open door.*)
No vulgar fear befits the daughter of high Zeus,
nor is she moved by panic's lightly-skimming touch.
What is this horror, from the womb of Chaos old,
approaching, hollow-eyed, blood-drenched, in haggard
height?
Look at her there! She ventures to confront the light!
But till the king shall come, we are the masters here.
(*MEPHISTOPHELES, as PHORKYAS, steps out onto the
threshold between the two door-posts.*)

CHORUS: I have seen many and terrible happenings;   40
warfare and anguish, night in the city,
as Troy fell.

Through the dust-clouded tumult of soldiers,
I heard the gods calling, brazen, discordant,
to the ramparts.

They were still standing, but flames were spreading
from neighbour to neighbourhood, borne by the firestorm
of its own creation, on through the city
benighted.

Then, as I fled, I saw, through the firelight's   50
flickering tongues on the smoke, come striding
figures of gods, gigantic, threatening
and terrible.

Did I see this, or did I
imagine what my fear called up?
I shall never know, but here
is a horror I can see,
touch it even, were it not
for the fear that holds me back
from danger.   60

PHORKYAS: The ancient saying holds; the sense is trite
but true,
that Beauty never yet went hand-in-hand with Shame.
You think it's hid from me, to what race you belong?

Begotten in the wars, in battle bred, a brood
lascivious, man-crazed, seducers and seduced,
sapping both the warrior's and the citizen's strength.
You locust swarm, swooped down to cover the green corn,
you greedy wasters of the toil of other men,
you loot of war, twice-bartered, damaged goods!

HELEN: To criticise the servant in the presence of   70
the mistress, is a theft of household privilege:
it is for her alone to hand out praise or blame.
She asks not what the servant is, but how he serves.
So hold your peace, lest you receive well-earned rebuke.

PHORKYAS: The right to threaten the domestic staff remains
a sacred right the wife will take long years to earn.
Since you, now recognised once more, resume your place
as queen and mistress, then take up the reins
so long neglected, and be ruler here of all
your treasures and possessions, us along with them.   80
But most of all, protect me, I who am the eldest,
from this pack that, beside the swan that is your beauty,
seem nothing but a clutch of ill-fledged, cackling geese.

HELEN: In sorrow, not in anger, do I intervene.
No greater harm befalls a monarch's state, than when
his servants quarrel secretly amongst themselves.
What images are these you have evoked? Is it
remembrance? madness? was I that? what am I now?
Must I be evermore the nightmare and the dream
of those who burn our towns and put them to the sword?   90

PHORKYAS: The average man is blessed with average
                          luck, and sees
the highest favour of the gods as just a dream.
But you, though you were favoured past all bounds, you
                          could
not see beyond the crowd surrounding you, in rut,
inflamed by lust to any reckless enterprise.
First Theseus, beautiful and strong as Heracles...

HELEN: ...abducted and imprisoned me, at ten years old.

PHORKYAS: Yet soon, by your twin brothers freed and set
                          at large,
a band of chosen heroes came to sue for you.

HELEN: My secret favours though, I willingly admit,   100
    Patroclus took, who was Achilles' greatest love.
PHORKYAS: Your father then to Menelaus married you.
    But while he fought in Crete, you entertained a guest.
HELEN: Oh, why recall the time of my half-widowhood,
    and all the ruin, horrible to me, it caused?
PHORKYAS: You left all this, allured by Ilium's topless towers,
    as well as by the inexhaustible lure of love.
HELEN: Don't call it that: the stark infinity of pain
    and of remorse has overwhelmed my heart and mind.
PHORKYAS: But still it's said you managed to appear in two   110
    distinct locations, both in Egypt and in Troy.
HELEN: Do not confuse a mind already too distraught;
    even now I do not know the truth of what I am.
PHORKYAS: It's also said Achilles made the journey here,
    from Hell, defying the laws of Fate, to lie with you!
HELEN: It was a dream, the very words confirm it was;
    I was a wraith, a ghost, a phantom, bound to another.
    And now – I faint, and to myself become a ghost.
    (*She swoons into the arms of the SEMI-CHORUS.*)
CHORUS: Silence! False of tongue and eye!
    From those one-toothed, hideous lips,   120
    only loathsome words can issue.

    Wolf in sheep's clothing, feigning charity,
    far more terrible to me
    than the jaws of Cerberus.

    Anxiously we stand here waiting.
    When? Where? How will this deep malice
    of this thing of Hell break out?

    Now, instead of comfort, you
    evoke the evil past, and darken
    present joy and future hope.   130

    Silence, then! that Helen's spirit,
    ready to escape, may firmly
    keep that form of fairest beauty
    that the sun has ever shone on.
    (*HELEN has meanwhile come to herself, and stands once
    more in their midst.*)

PHORKYAS: Now the sun comes fiercely striding,
                         from behind the rack of cloud.
     Even veiled we worshipped him,
                         who now in dazzling splendour reigns.
     As the world unrolls before you,
                         so your graceful glance revives.
     Though you all may call me hideous,
                         I know where true Beauty lies.
     Wake in Beauty! Stand in greatness!
                         Tell us what you would command.
HELEN: Then be ready to atone for all delays your quarrels
                                                  caused.   140
     Go, prepare the sacrifice that was commanded by your king.
PHORKYAS: All is ready in the palace: incense, tripod,
                                           sharpened axe,
     and the bowl to catch the offering. Let the victim now be
                                            named.
HELEN: That the king has left unspoken.
PIIORKYAS: Not revealed it? Dreadful news!
HELEN: What is this display of dread?
PHORKYAS: The victim, oh my Queen, is you!
HELEN: I?
PHORKYAS: And these here.
CHORUS: Gods have mercy!
PHORKYAS: You shall perish by the axe.
HELEN: Dreadful, yet not unsuspected.
PHORKYAS: Unavoidable, it seems.
CHORUS: What is to be our fate, then?
PHORKYAS: She will die a noble death.
     But for you – along the roof-beam,
                         like wet clothes hung out to dry.
     (*HELEN and the CHORUS stand carefully grouped to
     indicate terror and astonishment.*)
PENTHALIS: The Queen now stands apart, in contemplation
                                            rapt.   150

     The women droop like grass. On me, it seems
     the duty has devolved, as eldest here, with you,
     eldest of eldest, to exchange a word or two.

From your experience, wisdom, and seeming charity,
although this brainless bunch misjudged, and howled at you,
tell me, now, if you know, is rescue possible?
PHORKYAS: Soon said: upon the queen alone your fate
                          depends.
PENTHALIS: Speak, and tell us, tell us quickly,
  how may we avoid the dreadful fate
  above our heads impending?   160
PHORKYAS: The man who stays at home, who guards his
                      well-earned wealth,
  who can secure his roof against the attack of rain,
  all shall go well with him, through all his earthly days.
  But he who oversteps his threshold and departs,
  impelled to guilty acts, on his return,
  will find the old place changed, if not quite wrecked.
HELEN: What is the purpose of these outworn proverbs here?
  Say what you have to say, and leave offensive talk
PHORKYAS: The king spent ten long years before the walls
                      of Troy;
  how many more on the journey home, I do not know.   170
  Meanwhile how are things going in the royal house?
  And what is the condition of the country here?
HELEN: Can you not draw a breath without reproaching me?
PHORKYAS: Behind the mountains, in the valley there, a tribe
  of mettlesome invaders, from the Northern night,
  has settled, made their stronghold unassailable,
  from which they ravage land and people as they wish.
HELEN: How have they managed that? It seems impossible.
PHORKYAS: They have had ample time – well nigh on
                      twenty years.
HELEN: Is there one chief? Or are they brigands in alliance? 180
PHORKYAS: They are not brigands, and they do obey a
                      single lord.
HELEN: Describe him.
PHORKYAS: Courageous, cheerful, handsome and
                      well-built,
  blessed with a better mind than most men here in Greece.
  You call such folk barbarians, yet none, I think,
  is quite as savage as the heroes seen at Troy,

butchers, whose only pleasure lay in killing men.
This man has greatness, which I both respect and trust.
And round him moves a troop of youths, fresh, golden-
                                                    haired,
in the first flush and bloom of early manhood – such
as only Paris was, when he approached the queen...too
                                            close.   190

HELEN: Be quiet! That is not in your part. Speak your last
                                            word.

PHORKYAS: That is for you to speak: a clear, sincere 'yes',
    and I shall have you safe inside his castle walls.

CHORUS: Oh, say that one short word, and save yourself –
                                            and us.

HELEN: What? Can I suppose my husband, and your king,
    could ever be so savage as to do me harm?

PHORKYAS: Have you forgotten, after Paris had been killed,
    what he did to Deiphobus; Paris's brother, when
    he found he had successfully laid siege to your
    uncompromising widowhood. Chopped off his nose, his ears,   200
    and other mutilations – horrible to see.

HELEN: But he did that to *him* – he did it for my sake.

PHORKYAS: And now, for his own sake, he'll do the same
                                            to you.

    Beauty is not for sharing: he who's had it once
    destroys it sooner than go into partnership.
    Listen! The trumpets' blare assaults both ears and guts.
    So jealousy attacks the man who can't forget
    what he once had, and lost, which will not come again.

CHORUS: Can't you hear the trumpets blaring?
                        Can't you see the flash of steel?

PHORKYAS: Welcome to my King, and Master! Let me
                        make my reckoning.   210

CHORUS: What of us?

PHORKYAS: You know. Her murder
                        will take place before your eyes.
    And your own is waiting in there:
                        nothing more can save you now.

(*Pause.*)

HELEN: I have decided on the next step I shall take.
    You are a hostile demon; that is clear to me,
    and I fear you will subvert even this good to evil.
    However, I shall follow you to this retreat.
    I know the rest – but what the queen may choose to keep
    concealed in her most secret heart, let it remain
    a mystery to all for ever. Witch, lead on!
    (*Mists spread, covering the scene.*)

CHORUS: Sisters, see!   220
    What is this?
    Was it not day?
    The rising mist
    grows thicker still.
    We scarcely see
    each other now.
    What is happening?
    Are we floating?
    Are we waking?
    D'you see nothing?   230
    All at once the darkness deepens.
    Mist dissolves in skeins around us,
    murky, brown and grey. Like stonework
    walls rise up to meet our vision
    rise to barricade our vision.
    Is it courtyard? Is it quarry?
    Just as frightening, whichever.
    Sisters, we have been imprisoned!
    Worse off than we were before.

2: Inner courtyard of Faust's castle in the North

Surrounded by fantastic mediaeval buildings. A long train of pages and knights comes down the stairs, after which FAUST appears at the head of the staircase, in the costume of a mediaeval knight. He descends slowly and with dignity. He approaches: beside him is a man in chains.

FAUST: In place of solemn greeting, and a fitting
    and honourable welcome, I have brought you

a slave in fetters, whose neglected duty
made me neglect my own. This is my watchman,
whose quite extraordinary powers of vision
give him the task of watching from the tower
for any signs of movement on the horizon.
Today though – negligence and dereliction!
Your Highness's approach was not announced:
the honourable welcome due to such 10
a noble guest was lacking. For his crime,
his life is forfeit. He should by now be dead.
But you alone shall punish or show mercy.
HELEN: High is the honour you confer on me,
    even if only, as I must suspect,
    to put me to some test. I'll act the judge,
    and let the accused speak in his own defence.
LYNCEUS: Let me live and let me gaze;
    let me die or let me live;
    to this gift from God, I give 20
    all my service, all my days.

    Watching Eastward for the morn
    to break in glory over us,
    sudden and miraculous,
    in the South arose the dawn.

    I surrendered heart and mind.
    Eye and hand no more obeyed me.
    Her all-blinding beauty made me –
    lynx-eyed Lynceus – stone-blind.

    I forgot my watchman's duty, 30
    failed to blow the signal horn.
    Though your threats may kill me, scorn
    and anger will submit to Beauty.
HELEN: The evil that I caused I may not punish.
    Oh, what harsh destiny pursues me still,
    that makes men so infatuated that
    they lose all care, either of life or honour,
    but plunder, murder, quarrel and seduce?
    Demigods, heroes, gods, and demons too
    have led me to and fro, as in a maze. 40
    Now I heap trouble up on trouble's head.

      Take him away. He is innocent. The gods
      made him a fool, but not a criminal.
FAUST: My Queen, I have observed, in some amazement,
      the unerring archer, and her stricken mark.
      But what of me? One glance from you, and all
      my servants turn to rebels: my very walls
      are insecure – henceforth my armies will
      serve you alone, all-conquering, unconquered.
      Then what remains for me to do, except   50
      to yield myself; and all I thought was mine,
      to you, and to acknowledge you as queen?
LYNCEUS: (*With a coffer; followed by others with more.*)
      All I thought worthy to possess
      all reason, riches, thought and power,
      I lay before your beauty's flower –
      too conscious of my worthlessness.
FAUST: Remove yourself, unpunished, but unpraised.
      All that the castle holds is hers already;
      a special offer is superfluous.
      Heap treasure up in organised profusion;   60
      bring out glories yet unseen, and let
      the treasure-vaults flash into glittering life.
      Prepare a Paradise before her, so
      wherever her glance, that blinds all but the Gods,
      shall fall, it shall not fail to fall on Beauty.
LYNCEUS: You command me to my duty,
      yet I see it all as play.
      Riches, blood and heart obey
      the prodigality of Beauty.
      (*He goes out.*)
HELEN: Let me talk with you – but first assure   70
      my place for me, by taking yours as well.
FAUST: First, on my knees, let my allegiance be
      accepted; let me kiss the hand that raises
      me to your side; confirm me as co-regent
      of your infinite kingdom and win for yourself
      worshipper, slave and guardian all at once.
CHORUS: Nearer and nearer they draw together,
      leaning against one another,

shoulder to shoulder,
knee to knee,   80
hand in hand,
they rock and sway.
Not for royalty
to hide its pleasures,
but take them unblushing,
in front of the people.
FAUST: When longing grows too great, we cannot bear it;
    we look about us, asking...
HELEN: Who will share it?
FAUST: The soul seeks not what's past, nor what's to be;
    only the present moment...
HELEN: Holds our ecstasy.   90
FAUST: That is the treasure which we understand.
    What guarantees my claim to it?
HELEN: My hand.
    I feel so far away, and yet so near:
    I only long to say: 'Here – I am Here.'
FAUST: I hardly breathe; speech fails me, and I shiver
    in a dream where Space and Time are lost forever.
HELEN: I feel lived-out, and yet reborn, full-grown,
    inseparable from, and faithful to the Unknown.
FAUST: Ask not what lies behind Man's destiny;
    we are here, however briefly, just to be.   100
    (*He sits beside her. During the following lines FAUST and
    HELEN fly to Arcadia.*)
    To you, to me, Fate has been kind: the past
    is put behind us, all that's ever been.
    Be conscious of divine descent: at last
    you belong wholly to the primal scene.

    No fortress strong enough to hold you in:
    in everlasting youth and strength abide,
    for us and for our happiness to win,
    Arcadia and Sparta, side by side.

    In your flight to find safe harbour,
    you found happiest destiny.   110

Throne-room now be changed to arbour!
Arcadian our bliss, and free!
MEPHISTOPHELES: (*Entering brusquely; ad spectatores.*)
You've always been obsessed with watching love affairs,
caught, as you often are, in the same labyrinth.
But the next time you see this couple, in a moment,
they will be parents of a beautiful young boy.
Euphorion is his name – classical – don't ask why:
enough that he is there, though, in the manner of
those history plays where babes grow up, becoming heroes
in a few scenes – the going's even wilder here.   120
He's scarcely been conceived when he is born,
jumping around and dancing, fighting. Many people
criticise this, though others think it's not to be
taken at its face value, but has A Deeper Meaning.
They sense some mystery, mystification even,
on the Egyptian pattern, or the Indian:
and anyone whose pleasure it is to stir
up things like that, and delve into the brew
of etymology and such, is welcome to it.
For such men, we can only recommend   130
an earnest study of modern symbolism.
This is no longer any place for me.
The thread of narrative winds on its spooky way
to an unhappy ending. Hail and farewell!
Next time we meet, we'll both have much to tell.
(*He leaves.*)

3: The fields of Arcadia

The CHORUS lies scattered about, asleep.

HELEN: Love will join two hearts together,
    increase them to a precious three.
FAUST: All has been fulfilled. Forever
    may we know this ecstasy.
EUPHORION: Now I spring on solid earth,
    but the earth retaliates,
    throws me high up in the air:

with a second spring, a third,
throws me to the very roof.
FAUST: Caution, caution, a fatal fall   10
would bring sorrow to us all.
EUPHORION: I'll stay no longer
here on land.
Let go my clothes,
let go my hand.
HELEN: Gently, gently,
for our sake restrain
your impetuosity.
If you are lost to me,
joy that you bring to me   20
won't come again.
EUPHORION: For your sakes alone
I curb my flight.
(*He winds his way among the CHORUS, drawing them into
the dance.*)
Look! Is the tune
and the movement right?
HELEN: Yes – now advance:
create in the dance
graceful designs.
FAUST: I wish it were over. I
know such things threaten my   30
balance of mind.
EUPHORION: (*Pulling in a young GIRL.*)
See me pull this nymph to me:
I shall force her, let her see
who is master here, insist
on kissing that unwilling breast
and mouth. If she resists me still,
I'll let her feel my strength and will.
GIRL: Let me go! My body stores
strength and courage, just like yours:
our will's the equal of your own,   40
and not so easily overthrown.
Trusting much to your strong hand, you
thought I could not get away;

179

hold me tight, and I shall brand you,
stupid boy, and all in play.
(*She bursts into flame and flares up into the air.*)
Follow me through air and space,
follow me through deep crevasse,
try to catch your vanished prey!
EUPHORION: (*Shaking off the last of the flames.*)
Rocks all around I see,
woods that enmesh   50
and try to imprison me:
still I am young and fresh.
Storms, gales and tempests roar,
waves beat upon the shore;
all in my mind I hear.
if only I were there!
I must climb up higher, higher,
and a wider world survey.
(*He bounds higher and higher up the crags.*)
HELEN: Why such passion to aspire
beyond a world that bids you stay?   60
CHORUS: Poetry, rise
to hallowed skies!
Shine out, bright star,
further off than afar:
beauty and artistry,
for these we should always be
glad – and we are.
EUPHORION: Now I am a child no longer,
but a man in arms I come,
joined with the freer, braver, stronger,   70
marching to a distant drum;
yonder lie
the battles I
must snatch my fame and glory from.
HELEN: Scarcely called to life, and scarcely
given to the cheerful day,
you desert us both, perversely
choosing the most painful way.
Are we two

nothing to you   80
but a dream of yesterday?
EUPHORION: Listen! The thunder on the ocean
echoes closer, on the land.
Spray and dust confound confusion,
army fights army, clashes hand to hand.
Death, at the end,
is in command,
this suddenly I understand.
HELEN/FAUST/CHORUS: Oh, the horror! This is
                                  nightmare!

Are you singled out for Death?   90
EUPHORION: Shall I stay safe out of sight here,
or share their troubles while I've breath?
HELEN/FAUST/CHORUS: Arrogance brings
Death in its train.
EUPHORION: Nothing restrains
me – now, I have wings.
Do not begrudge me this,
but go I must.
(*He launches himself into the air. For a moment his clothes
hold him up, his head shines and a trail of light follows him.*)
CHORUS: Icarus! Icarus!
Now he is dust.   100
(*A beautiful boy falls at their feet. We think we recognise in
the dead a well-known figure but the body vanishes at once,
the aureole rising to Heaven like a comet. Clothes, mantle
and lyre are left lying on the ground.*)
FAUST/HELEN: All the earthly joy we know
by pain is quickly overthrown.
EUPHORION: (*A voice from the depths.*)
Mother, do not let me go
into darkness all alone.
(*A pause, then the CHORUS begins a lament.*)
CHORUS: Not alone! Your soul is straying
into worlds we may not know.
Though on earth you found no staying,
our hearts will not let you go.

Envy's voice may join together
with our own, to mourn your fate: 110
but, in fair and bitter weather,
both your heart and song were great.

Born to fortune, name and power,
all the blessings of this earth;
soon, too soon, your early flower
was crushed before it knew its worth.
Eyes, that saw the world so clearly;
sympathy with every wrong;
heart, that women loved so dearly;
and a unique, unshared song.   120

But you ran, unhesitating,
to the net that snares the mind,
arrogantly violating
custom and the law combined.
Then, at last, that noble spirit
lent your courage gravity:
you wished glory to inherit –
but, for you, it could not be.

Then for whom? Predestination
furnishes no clear reply;   130
while in pain and desolation
nations mutely bleed and die.
But sing out once more! and end a
life of slavery in the span.
Old earth will new songs engender,
as she has since Time began.
(*Long pause. The music fades.*)
HELEN: (*To FAUST.*)

An ancient proverb has, alas, come true in me:
Beauty and Happiness cannot stay long together.
My link with Life is snapped, as is the chain of Love.
Regretting both, I take a sorrowful farewell,   140
throwing myself in your embrace for one last time.
Persephone, Queen of Hell, now take my child, and me.
(*She embraces FAUST. Her body vanishes, her dress and veil
remaining in his arms.*)

MEPHISTOPHELES: Hold on to all that's left of what you
had!
Don't let it go! Already, demons are
trying to drag it down into the shades.
Hold on to it! Even if it is not
the goddess whom you lost, it is still god-like.
A priceless gift, to bear you through the air
above all crude reality, as long
as you can stand the pace. We'll meet again,   150
but far, oh very far indeed, from here.
(*HELEN's garments dissolve into clouds. They envelop FAUST,
raising him aloft and carrying him away. MEPHISTOPHELES
picks up EUPHORION's clothes, mantle and lyre, and steps
forward to the proscenium, holding up the spoils and speaking to
the audience.*)
Now this is what I call a lucky find.
The sacred flame's gone out, but to my mind,
that's nothing to lose too much sleep about.
Enough is left to give the bards a lift,
which will ensure that colleagues will fall out;
and if the talent isn't in my gift,
at least I can still hire the wardrobe out.

End of Act Three.

ACT FOUR

1: Mountain heights

A bleak, jagged mountain summit. A cloud approaches, clinging to the rock, then settles on a projecting ledge. The cloud divides and FAUST steps out of it.

FAUST: Gazing down, I see the deepest solitude
　　as I step thoughtfully along this mountain ridge.
　　My chariot of cloud dismissed – it floats away
　　towards the East, changing as it glides,
　　taking the shape...it is no optical illusion!
　　A gigantic yet beautiful female form – a Juno,
　　a Leda, or a Helen. Now it scatters – still
　　a rack of cloud floats round me. Am I deluded
　　into thinking it the highest, most longed-for good
　　of youth? The deepest, earliest treasures of the heart　　10
　　well up – light-winged, and bringing back Aurora's love;
　　that first glance, quickly felt but scarcely understood,
　　which, while I held it fast, surpassed all other treasures.
　　Like the soul's beauty now the lovely form ascends
　　into the air, yet still it keeps its shape
　　and all the better part of me it bears away.
　　(*A seven-league boot clomps onto the stage, followed immediately by another. MEPHISTOPHELES descends. The boots stride offstage in haste.*)
MEPHISTOPHELES: So – *there* you are. You've led me
　　　　　　　　　　　　　　　　quite a chase.
　　But why on earth bring me to this vile place?
　　I recognise it, though: I knew it well:
　　this used to be the very floor of Hell,　　20
　　before God tumbled Satan from his throne
　　and turned all of creation upside down.
FAUST: The hills loom up on either side of me,
　　silencing speculation of how they came to be.
MEPHISTOPHELES: 'In this exceeding high place',
　　　　　　　　　　　　　　　where, unfurled

before you, 'lay all the kingdoms of this world,
and the glory of them' – as you see, I can
quote it like any ordinary man –
was there no temptation you could find
for you and your enquiring mind?   30
FAUST: Yes. A vast idea led me on.
MEPHISTOPHELES: Sublime, no doubt. Since you're so
near the moon,
d'you mean to travel there?
FAUST: No, I do not.
This earth still gives me ample scope for what
I have in mind, astonishing, bold and new.
I feel the strength in me to see it through.
MEPHISTOPHELES: A lust for glory? It is plain to see
that you've been keeping heroines company.
FAUST: I shall achieve both power and property:
the deed, and not the fame is all that counts for me.   40
MEPHISTOPHELES: Yet authors will be found, to praise
your actions to all future days –
fools teaching fools, in foolish ways.
FAUST: Hidebound spirit, can you start
to know what stirs the human heart?
Creature of bitter, contrary breed,
what can you know of human need?
MEPHISTOPHELES: Let it be done according to Thy
word – on earth.
What new caprice is this that we must bring to birth?
FAUST: My eyes were drawn towards the mighty ocean: 50
I saw it, surging, swelling more and more,
setting its waves into triumphant motion
and flinging them in thunder on the shore.
Depressing. It reminded me of how
the free untrammelled spirit can allow
itself to be beaten down by arrogance,
provoked into unwilling intemperance.
Coincidence, I thought; then looked again
more closely at the wave. It paused, and then,
back from its proudly-won goal, the wave retreated.   60
But time comes round, the old game is repeated...

MEPHISTOPHELES: (*Ad spectatores.*)
    Not quite the latest news to reach my ears:
    something I've known for several million years.
FAUST: (*Continuing with passion.*)
    ...and in through a thousand channels creeps the sea,
    sterile itself, spreading sterility.
    Over the desolate waste the waves sweep on
    and back again – and nothing has been done.
    It could drive one to despair, so to survey
    how mindless elements hold pointless sway.
    I wondered – how to bring it in control?   70
    I formed a plan, and it is possible.
    However high the tide, it always will
    go round even the smallest obstacle.
    A slight height will deflect it from its course,
    a slight depression will attract its force.
    Plan grew on plan: what triumph it would be
    if we could find means to confine the sea
    within a man-made boundary! What I planned
    was no less than reclamation of the land.
    I could explain how, step by step, it is connected: 80
    now you must have the courage to effect it.
    (*Drums and military music heard in the distance, to the right*
    at the back of the audience.)
MEPHISTOPHELES: Child's play – do you hear the
                               distant drum?
FAUST: The wise man worries when the soldiers come.
MEPHISTOPHELES: Peace – war – who cares? The wise
                            man will take care
    in whichever case, to grab his proper share;
    eye the main chance, till it becomes a habit.
    Faust, your chance has come! Step up and grab it!
FAUST: Just tell me what I have to do, and spare me
    your usual conundrums – state things clearly!
MEPHISTOPHELES: On my way here I gleaned some
                           information 90
    about the Emperor's current, parlous situation.
    Remember him? We helped him, in a fix,
    with paper currency and conjuring tricks.

So much so he began to think he owned
the whole world – he was very young when crowned.
Now he has nearly bankrupted the palace, he
has fallen victim to the dangerous fallacy
that it's both possible and right,
two incompatibles to unite,
to govern *and* to indulge one's appetite.   100
FAUST: A grave mistake. Whoever must command, must be
a man whose sole delight is in authority.
With his high will his heart and mind are full,
but what he wills remains unfathomable.
He whispers his intent in trusted ears – it's done!
The world's amazed, and he stands second to none.
Nothing is more degrading than enjoyment.
MEPHISTOPHELES: The quest for pleasure was his sole
                                                employment.
Empire had collapsed in anarchy,
and general, mutual hostility.   110
High and low were ranged against each other;
brother persecuted and slaughtered brother;
castle fought castle, city attacked city:
even the Church shared in the atrocity.
All men were enemies. Living was little more
than self-defence. And that is how the score
stood until lately. Since there was no
strong central government, the strongest rose
to say: 'The Emperor must be deposed.
Since he cannot ensure peace, we must choose   120
another, who will bring new life to the land,
protecting subjects of every station,
in a new-created nation,
where Peace and Justice go hand in hand.'
FAUST: I smell religion.
MEPHISTOPHELES: Oh yes, there were priests,
taking good care of their own interests.
They were more implicated than the rest. It
seemed the more unrest grew, the more they blessed it.
Meanwhile the Emperor, whom we'd amused,

bemused, confused, bamboozled in the past, 130
prepares for battle – probably his last.
FAUST: I'm sorry for him – too naif and open.
MEPHISTOPHELES: Let's watch a little: while there's life
there's hope, and
who can tell just how the dice will fall?
(*They cross over the central mountain-range and survey the
drawing-up of the army in the valley. The sound of drums
and military bands comes up from below.*)
The strategical position's good, and all
he needs for victory is our intervention.
Think of your recent laudable intention.
If we preserve the Emperor's throne, and land,
you kneel to him, and as reward, demand
possession of the boundless coastal strand. 140
FAUST: After all you've already done,
now show me how a battle's won.
MEPHISTOPHELES: No, that's for you to do; to show
yourself an expert generalissimo.
(*He gives a piercing whistle.*)
FAUST: Just the promotion that I need – I can't
command where I'm completely ignorant.
MEPHISTOPHELES: The General Staff can do it all,
so the General's safe whate'er befalls:
he can sit back behind the line
knowing that things are working out just fine, 150
and that whatever the result may be,
he needn't take responsibility.
The hell of war's an old cliché:
the war of Hell's now on the way.
(*Enter three MIGHTY MEN.*)
Here come my pretty lads, assembled by my genius:
as you see, of different ages.
Their outfits may be somewhat miscellaneous,
but you will find they're worth their wages.
(*Ad spectatores.*)
Every child is glad to see
men in armour like these three; 160

and though these oafs are allegories,
that makes them likelier still to please.
WHACKER: (*Young, lightly-armed, colourful costume.*)
Smash him straight between the eyes,
and kill the coward as he flies.
SACKER: (*Manly, well-armed, rich costume.*)
Don't waste time in vain pursuit;
get in there and grab the loot.
PACKER: (*Elderly, heavily-armed, no costume.*)
Spendthrift brute and crass go-getter!
Taking's good, but keeping's better.
(*They descend together.*)

2: In the foothills

Drums and military music from below. The EMPEROR's tent is being pitched.

GENERAL: It seems the best available course
to choose the valley as a starting-place
where we can withdraw and amass our force,
and hope we shan't be losing face.
EMPEROR: We shall soon see. But, victory or defeat,
I don't like this withdrawal, this half-retreat.
GENERAL: Your Majesty, our right-hand flank's position
would satisfy the fussiest tactician.
Hill not too steep, nor too accessible,
good for us, for the foe well nigh impossible.   10
Half-hidden in the plain, hills at our back,
their cavalry will never dare attack.
EMPEROR: What can I offer but congratulations?
Now let our courage be equal to the occasion.
GENERAL: Here stands, just where our centre comes in sight,
our troops' main body, itching for the fight.
The early sunshine, piercing the morning haze,
gilds their splendid weapons with its rays.
In a dark mass now stirs the mighty square,
thousands of men, on fire to do and dare.   20

189

The big battalions, Majesty, are what we
trust most in to destroy the enemy.
EMPEROR: I never saw so fine a sight before;
an army with the strength of ten, or more.
GENERAL: Of our left flank there is not much to tell.
Our heroes hold the sheer cliffs here as well.
This rocky height here, now armed to the teeth,
controls the entrance to the pass beneath.
And here, where none expect a bloody battle,
we can butcher all their men like so much cattle.   30
FIRST SCOUT: We have carried out our mission
with both cunning craft and courage.
We penetrated their position,
but bring back little to encourage.
Although your allies solemnly swore
loyal oaths, they nonetheless protest
inaction is the very best
way to keep out of civil war.
EMPEROR: The selfish man's inevitable attitude,
blind to all duty, honour, friendship, gratitude.   40
Can they not realise, when the bill falls due,
their neighbour's fire may reach their own house too?
SECOND SCOUT: At first we were relieved to see
disorder in their state of war,
suddenly, unexpectedly,
arose a rival Emperor.
Armies now at his behest
under his false banner, sweep
through the land, and all the rest
follow – as usual – like silly sheep.   50
EMPEROR: A man's self is the man: he who wears a crown
must prove himself worthy to occupy his throne.
Let this presumptuous ogre, this pretender,
this self-styled emperor, and realm's defender,
let him now be uprooted from my land,
and hurled to death by my Imperial hand.
(*HERALDS are despatched to offer challenge to the ANTI-EMPEROR.*

Enter FAUST, in armour; with half-closed visor, attended
by the three MIGHTY MEN, dressed as before.)

FAUST: Whether the situation will improve or worsen,
    Your Majesty is wrong to expose his royal person.
    Without a head, what can the body do?
    If the head sleeps, the body must sleep too.   60
    If the head's off, the body can't survive.
    Only a healthy head keeps it alive.

GENERAL: Forward our right wing! The enemy's objective,
    our men, young, fit and tried, will render ineffective.

FAUST: Accept this man of might, then, at your side,
    and let his quality be quickly tried.

WHACKER: Anyone coming at me today,
    leaves with his head half shot away:
    enemy dead, behind, before,
    shall welter in their own vile gore.   70
    (*He goes out.*)

GENERAL: Now have the centre column march in force
    to halt the enemy in his fatal course!

FAUST: Then let this splendid hero be
    enrolled in your ranks immediately!

SACKER: The army's pride's no substitute
    for a healthy appetite for loot:
    I'll lead the men, on plunder bent,
    right to the rival emperor's tent.

STACKER: (*A camp-follower nestling up to him.*)
    Though I never wed the lad,
    he's the best lay I ever had.   80
    The harvest's ripe, as never before;
    women are red in tooth and claw,
    when loot's around, they know no law –
    press on! all's fair in love and war.
    (*They go out together.*)

GENERAL: Their right falls on our left: our men push back
    the fury of their treacherous attack.

FAUST: Consider this man too. It can't be wrong
    to strengthen even what's already strong.

PACKER: About the left wing, have no further care:
    possession is assured if I am there.   90

An old man's strength is in his property;
nothing and no one can get that from me.
(*He goes out.*)

MEPHISTOPHELES: Now then, cast a backward glance,
and see a mighty host advance,
with helmet, armour, shield and spear,
to form a rampart in our rear,
waiting to start its bloody task.
Where I got them from? Don't ask.
Recruited them in rapid stages
from ghosts, brought back to play the Middle Ages!   100
Knights, emperors, kings they may have been before;
now they are empty snail-shells, nothing more.
Still, stick a demon or two within;
I have no further doubt we'll win.

EMPEROR: On the darkening horizon,
where I saw one before, I see a dozen.

ARCHBISHOP: Something here's unnatural.

EMPEROR: Things aren't going well at all.
Look, our front line's falling back
before the enemy attack!   110
We've already lost the pass.
The enemy presses on, *en masse.*
You've lost my war for me!

ARCHBISHOP: All this
is the consequence of blasphemies.

EMPEROR: So at last I am betrayed –
and by servants! You all laid
snares to catch me in your net.

MEPHISTOPHELES: Courage! All's not lost – not yet.
The hardest is the final stand.
Give order that I take command.   120

GENERAL: You chose these allies, Majesty,
a source of great distress to me –
their tricks should quickly have been sat on.

EMPEROR: General! General! Keep your hat on!

GENERAL: I can't change things now – who can?
So let them end where they began:
please accept my marshal's baton.

EMPEROR: Keep it against some better day
    which destiny perhaps will send:
    (I do not trust him anyway,   130
    and even less his sinister friend.)
    (*To MEPHISTOPHELES.*)
    Sir, I am trying to be impartial.
    You aren't the type to make Field-Marshal,
    but – if you've an idea that can
    save the Empire – you're our man.
    (*He goes into his tent, with the GENERAL.*)
FAUST: What will you do?
MEPHISTOPHELES: It's all as good as done.
    Spirits of Water, use your high, mysterious art
    to set Appearance and Reality apart.
    (By feminine arts, obscure and hard to know,
    they understand how to separate the two,   140
    so that all swear that what they see and feel
    is there, but it's illusion, quite unreal.)
    Send the appearance of a raging torrent
    against the enemy – not an actual current,
    but one they'll take for real, and fly in panic.
FAUST: Listen!
MEPHISTOPHELES: Already?
FAUST: Downwards a titanic
    wall of water rushes and engulfs
    horses and men. They try to save themselves.
    Even the bravest fly – in vain; the wall
    crashes down on them, and destroys them all,   150
    plunging in terror to the gulf below.
MEPHISTOPHELES: I can't see any of all that, you know.
    The illusion only works on human eyes.
    Still, one can't watch it without some surprise.
    Look at them, thinking that they're being drowned,
    retching and choking, when they're safe and sound
    and swimming madly along, on bone-dry ground.
    Thick darkness over them is spreading,
    they cannot see where they are heading;
    deluding flashes everywhere   160
    blind them with a sudden glare.

All this has beautifully succeeded,
but now some greater terror's needed.
FAUST: Is now the time to deploy your hosts
of hollow mediaeval ghosts?
Exhumed from armoury and sepulchre,
they quicken, snuffing up the open air,
clattering, jangling, steel on bone,
an unreal, wild, discordant tone.
MEPHISTOPHELES: Good! They can no longer be
restrained!   170

The ancient chivalry they once contained
stirs into life. The spectres clank and rattle,
keen to renew their old, eternal battle.

In the Devil's interest,
party-hatred works the best,
and will, till honour ends it all.

Now, upon these sounds of rout,
panic scream and hellish shout,
let us let the curtain fall.

3: The rival Emperor's tent

Throne, luxurious trappings.

SACKER: (*Entering with his whore.*)
We were the first ones here, you see.
STACKER: No bird can fly as fast as we.
SACKER: The place was loaded fit to burst.
STACKER: I didn't know what to pick up first.
SACKER: (*Picking up a weapon.*)
With this the job is quickly done:
just crack their skulls and pass along.
But you've got far too much to pack.
There's nowt but rubbish in that sack.
Leave it behind with all the rest,
and grab hold of that little chest.   10
STACKER: Why, what's in it anyway?
SACKER: Only all the army's pay.

STACKER: It's such a weight, I'll never shift it.

Look at me, I can't even lift it.

SACKER: Bend down, then. Quick! I'll give a hoist.

You've had more on your back than most.

STACKER: I'm done for! Will you never learn? Ya

Just gave me a double hernia!

Oh, God, I'm dying! You hear that crack?

I think the chest just broke my back   20

(*The chest falls and splits open.*)

SACKER: It's lying there in a great big heap.

STACKER: (*Crouching down.*)

Hurry! Sweep it into my lap.

That's enough, we can't take it all.

SACKER: Oh, no! Your apron's got a hole.

GUARD: (*Of the real EMPEROR.*)

What are you people doing here?

This belongs to the Emperor.

SACKER: We risked our lives dirt cheap before;

now we're taking the spoils of war.

They're known as soldier's perks: just you

remember we were soldiers too.   30

GUARD: Soldiers under the Emperor's orders

are not a troop of wild marauders.

The men who serve His Majesty,

should all be honest soldiery.

SACKER: Oh, honesty! We know your game;

'requisitioning' – that's the name.

You're all the same, the way you're made:

'Hand over''s the motto of your trade.

(*To STACKER.*)

Take what you've got and leave the rest;

They're just about to speed the parting guest.   40

(*They leave. The GUARDS withdraw as the EMPEROR enters with his retinue.*)

EMPEROR: Magic or not, the day is ours: the foe is shattered!

Over the battlefield, his fleeing troops are scattered.

On every side the news is good, and better by the hour.

A peaceful Empire re-acknowledges our power.

What if a little jiggery-pokery was involved?

Finally on us responsibility devolved
to win the war alone. The fallen foe now lies,
an object of contempt, while we, proud victor, raise
our voice in praise of God, who gives such victories.
While all our subjects, in spontaneous exuberance,   50
raise a *Te Deum laudamus* for our deliverance.
ARCHBISHOP: My thanks, indeed the thanks of all, are
                                        due to the throne:
strengthening our power, you fortify your own.
EMPEROR: Now I dismiss you: let each go his separate way
to meditate upon the glories of this day.
(*All withdraw except the ARCHBISHOP.*)
ARCHBISHOP: I seek an audience with you, Sire, not as
                                        your chancellor,
but as your apprehensive spiritual counsellor.
Urged by a father's anxious care...
EMPEROR: I might have known you'd find
something to cloud the day. What is it on your mind?
ARCHBISHOP: With what a bitter pang, I find, in such an
                                        hour,   60
the Lord's Anointed dealing with the Satanic power.
Your throne's secure once more; yet this has been, alas,
achieved in mockery of God and of His Holiness,
who, when apprised of it, will scarcely hesitate
one second to declare you excommunicate.
Indeed, the ritual pronouncing of anathe-
ma is all you can expect now from the Holy Father.
But beat your repentant breast, and from your godless gain
give Holy Mother Church a modicum back again.
That broad hill-district, where your camp was lately pitched,   70
where your too-credulous ear by Satan was bewitched,
where you invoked assistance from the Prince of Lies,
consecrate it to some sacred enterprise.
Contrition, thus expressed, finds favour in God's eyes.
EMPEROR: My heavy fault appals me when I think of it.
Impose whatever heavy penance you think fit.
ARCHBISHOP: First, where the sin was done, the
                                        desecrated spot
must be reconsecrated to Almighty God.

In my mind's eye the noble walls rise higher and higher;
rays of the morning sun already gild the choir; 80
the great cathedral grows, transept and nave, in height
and length and breadth, to fill the faithful with delight.
Across the land rings out a mighty peal of bells,
and through the massive doors the congregation swells.
At the feast of dedication – which, let us hope, will be
solemnised in the not too distant future – we
expect the honoured presence of Your Majesty.
EMPEROR: If this great work will serve to fortify the nation
in Christian faith, that is sufficient expiation.
Enough! My burdened soul already seems more free. 90
ARCHBISHOP: As Chancellor, I require one more formality;
a title-deed to make the Church's rights secure.
EMPEROR: See that it's brought to me at once, for signature.
ARCHBISHOP: (*Having taken his leave, turns at the door.*)
One other thing: the Church will need a guarantee
of income from the land, in perpetuity –
all rents, rates, taxes, tithes. The upkeep needs
money and careful running, which makes for overheads.
Part of your war-loot, I imagine, you'll devote
to speed the building in a district so remote.
Moreover we shall need – this I cannot disguise – 100
timber and stone, and lime, and other such supplies,
to be brought from far away; transporting it shall be
the people's task; if preached at, they'll do it willingly.
The just man shall no longer live by faith alone:
the Church still blesses him who makes her tasks his own.
(*He leaves.*)
EMPEROR: My sin was great – the atonement is equally
extensive.
Those sorcerers turned out infernally expensive.
ARCHBISHOP: (*Returning yet again, with a deep bow.*)
Forgive me, Sire – you granted to… That Infamous Man
all coastal rights: but he will fall under the ban
of Holy Mother Church, unless in a frank, free 110
spirit of penitence, Your Majesty there too
will guarantee the Church a steady revenue
of rents, tithes, income, rates, and other taxes due.

EMPEROR: (*Peevishly.*)
>There's no land there: it's all miles out to sea.

ARCHBISHOP: Time is on the side of Patience and of
>>>>>>>>Wisdom.

>Your Majesty's word is still sufficient guarantee.

EMPEROR: (*Alone.*)
>If this goes on, I'll soon have signed away the kingdom.

End of Act Four.

ACT FIVE

1: Open country

WANDERER: Yes. They are the same old trees,
    grown so tall, so strong, with age,
    which this weary traveller sees
    after his long pilgrimage.

    Over there, quite close at hand,
    stands the hut that sheltered me,
    when the tempest-shaken sea
    cast me up upon the land.

    Where today's the honest pair
    who received me in their care?   10
    Shall I see them once again?
    No – they were old already then.

    Still, I'll call – perhaps they'll come.
    Is there anyone at home!
    (*Enter BAUCIS, a little, very old woman.*)
BAUCIS: Softly, stranger dear, my man
    has to sleep now when he can.
WANDERER: Mother, is it you? Still here!
    Now at last can man and wife
    take my thanks for all the care
    they took to save a stranger's life?   20

    Are you Baucis, who once filled
    a dead man's mouth with food and drink?
    (*The HUSBAND enters.*)
    And you, Philemon, who once pulled
    a dead man from the ocean's brink?

    No! First let me stand apart,
    and look out on the boundless seas,
    to try if prayer will bring some ease
    to my over-burdened heart.
    (*He walks up onto the dunes.*)

PHILEMON: Quickly, go and set the table
    underneath the shady trees: 30
    let him be; he's not yet able
    to believe the things he sees.
    (*Rejoins the WANDERER.*)
    Where we snatched you from the sea,
    and the tempest's raging tide,
    now stands a community;
    gardens flower on every side.

    Daring serfs obeyed their clever
    master, digging trenches and
    raising dykes, which served to sever
    sea from shore, and make new land.   40

    Now far out the ships are moving,
    seeking port at close of day.
    You find it hard, I see, believing
    that the sea's so far away;
    and here, where all was water, see!
    people are living happily.
    (*In the garden, the three at table.*)
BAUCIS: Try to eat a little. Come!
    And you haven't said a word.
PHILEMON: You like talking: tell him some
    of the amazing things we've heard.   50
BAUCIS: Yes; amazing is the word:
    gives me shivers still today.
    Miracles may have occurred,
    but not in any natural way.
PHILEMON: Did the Emperor do wrong to
    grant That Man that stretch of sand?
    It was broadcast through the land,
    he was the one it now belonged to.
BAUCIS: Work started by the very dune
    where we found you first – and soon   60
    green fields, and That Man's great house
    grew up right in front of us.

    The men worked hard while it was light,
    though it was labour thrown away:

but where the watch-fires burned at night,
you'd see a finished work next day.

Human beings must have died there;
we could hear their cries at night.
But at ebbing of the fiery tide, there
shone a canal in morning light.   70

That Man is godless. He respects
nothing: now he wants our home.
Says he's our neighbour, but he's come
to put his foot upon our necks.
PHILEMON: Still, he offered us a choice
of houses on the reclaimed land.
BAUCIS: That marsh! Not at any price:
up here we know where we stand.
PHILEMON: The little chapel bell is tolled,
to tell us of the end of day.   80
Let us go to kneel and pray
to God, to whom we prayed of old.

2: Palace – large ornamental garden – broad straight canal

FAUST, in extreme old age, walking about and brooding. From the dunes the bell can be heard ringing.

FAUST: (*With a start.*)
Damned bell! Humiliating sound,
like a treacherously-given wound!
In front – I rule, far as the eye can see:
behind – vexation is still dogging me.
Those mocking chimes remind me, my estate,
however mighty, is not yet complete.
The church, the orchard and their little home,
I cannot properly yet call my own.
If I should go there to refresh
myself, strange shadows would alarm me there;   10
thorns lie both underfoot and in the flesh.
Oh! if I could just be far away from here!

(*A magnificent barge ties up, with a rich and colourful cargo,*
from all corners of the world. The cargo is unloaded.
MEPHISTOPHELES and the three MIGHTY MEN appear.)

MEPHISTOPHELES: The way you look, it hardly seems
 your fortune exceeds man's wildest dreams.
 Your grand design has gone as planned:
 the sea's divorced now from the land.
 Out of the port, the argosies
 sweep swiftly over friendly seas.
 Here, in the palace, give the word
 and it is heard around the world.   20
 And here's where it began! Think back –
 here stood the little wooden shack –
 and this is where we dug the first
 canal – where fleets are now dispersed.
 Your people's strength, your grandiose plan
 reclaimed the land for use by Man.
 And here...

FAUST: That word! That damned word! *Here*!
 That is the word I cannot bear.
 I say to you, who'll understand it,
 it sears my mind like stabbing flame: 30
 I find I can no longer stand it;
 nor do I say this without shame.
 That aged couple must give in!
 I am the richest man on earth,
 but if those few trees are not mine,
 the rest is not of the slightest worth.
 I planned to build a belvedere
 among the trees, to give a view
 of all I have accomplished here:
 at one glance, able to review   40
 the masterpiece of human thought
 expressed in action – how I'd brought
 Nature under my master-plan,
 and won new living-space for Man.
 A rich man's fiercest torture is
 to know that something is not his.
 That chime, that scent of trees in bloom

wall me up here as in a tomb.
How may I drive out this chagrin?
Stop that infuriating din!   50
The omnipotence of my free will
is broken on that sandy hill.
Mulishness and selfishness
can spoil the most achieved success;
the pain, the rage and the disgust
force one to tire of being just.
MEPHISTOPHELES: Why trouble yourself with such a
                                                scruple?
Colonising means shifting people.
FAUST: Then go and shift that aged pair
into the house I gave them there.   60
Resettle them. It's in your care.
MEPHISTOPHELES: We'll pick them up and put them down,
before they even know they've gone.
A pretty home wall soon atone
for any violence that's been done.
(*He gives a piercing whistle: the three MIGHTY MEN come
forward.*)
(*Ad spectatores.*)
Not the first time in History it's been done:
see Naboth's vineyard, I Kings 21.

3: Midnight in the Palace

LYNCEUS: (*The Keeper of the Tower, sings from his watch post.*)
For vision begotten,
for watching employed,
my oath unforgotten,
the world I enjoyed.

I saw what was far,
I saw what was near,
moon, planet and star,
stream, forest and deer.

In all things I saw,
I found endless delight,   10

and delighted, the more
that they glutted my sight.

Oh, fortunate creature!
Such things I have seen,
whatever the future,
how fair it has been!

But I do not watch up here
for pleasure only. Listen! Sounds
of threatening horror, cries of fear
come from the darkness all around.   20
Sparks of fire I can see, flaring
from the orchard's double night;
fanned by winds, the flames are glaring
with an even fiercer light.
Now the cabin is ignited;
the mossy roof begins to burn.
The aged couple trapped inside it
do not know which way to turn.
No rescue for the poor old folk,
so good, so generous, so kindly –   30
in the midst of fire and smoke
they are left to perish blindly.
All is now a mass of flame,
the hut a charred and blackened frame.
Now the chapel's set alight
and collapses with the weight
of fallen, flaming branches – why
am I cursed with my all-seeing eye?
All dies down to a cinder-glow
and goes out. It is over now.   40
(*Long pause. Then he sings.*)
Those sights that gave delight and ease
are one now with the centuries.
FAUST: (*On the balcony, overlooking the dunes.*)
My watchman whimpers up above,
while I am gnawed by feelings of
vexation at the excessive haste.
Still, though the orchard's been laid waste,

we can at last make use of this to
create our unrestricted vista.
Meanwhile a new dwelling raise,
where the old devoted couple,   50
generously screened from trouble,
may enjoy their sunset days.
(*MEPHISTOPHELES with the three MIGHTY MEN
below.*)
MEPHISTOPHELES: We're back again: please understand,
but things got rather out of hand.
We knocked, and shouted for them to let us
in, but they would not admit us.
We rattled and knocked; the rotten door
lay in splinters on the floor.
We shouted warnings, loud and clear –
but none's so deaf as will not hear.   60
So, without any more ado,
we dragged them out, as ordered to.
The pain can only have been slight –
and brief; they must have died of fright.
A stranger, hiding in the hut,
resisted, so we killed him. But
in this brief, but brutal fight,
some live coals caught the straw alight.
Now the whole area is on fire,
and all three share one funeral-pyre.   70
FAUST: You turned deaf ears to my commands and me!
I meant exchange, not robbery!
I am appalled by this. I wish to see no more of you.
Wages? My curse! – share it amongst the four of you.
(*They go out, leaving FAUST alone on the balcony.*)
The stars are dim, the fire burns low,
the rising wind contrives to blow
the reek of smoke towards me now.
It was a rash command, I know,
but rashly executed, though.
(*Four GREY WOMEN approach.*)
What are you shadows hovering there?   80

WANT: Want.

NEED: Need.

DEBT: Debt.

CARE: Care.

WANT: The doors are all bolted.

DEBT: We cannot get in.

NEED: A rich man lives in there: we don't care for him.

WANT: There, Want's just a phantom.

NEED: Need ceases to be.

DEBT: And Want is a thing the rich never see.

CARE: Sisters, you don't dare, or don't care to go in,
    but Care can get in through the hole of a pin.
    (*CARE vanishes.*)

WANT: Sisters grey, let us away!

DEBT: But by your side, Debt will always stay.

NEED: And Need's as much a part of you as breath.   90

WANT: Drifting cloud and fading star:
    yonder, yonder, from afar,
    comes our brother.

DEBT: Coming.

NEED: Death.
    (*They go out.*)

FAUST: Four came in, but only three went hence.
    I heard them speak, but could not catch the sense.
    There was a word like 'Debt', and then I heard
    only a ghostly, faint, half-rhyming word
    like 'Death'. My struggle is not over yet.
    Could I abjure this magic, and forget
    its spells! If I could only stand again,   100
    a man, alone, and face to face
    with Nature, then it could be worth the pain
    we feel as members of the human race:
    such as I was, before I probed the occult,
    cursing Mankind and myself with the result.
    Superstition ensnares us, night and morning,
    when each event's a portent or a warning.
    We're helpless, scared, abandoned and alone.
    The door creaks – no one enters.

(*Shuddering.*)

                                  Who's there? Anyone?

CARE: Question expecting the answer 'Yes'; that's clear.   110

FAUST: And you, who are you then?

CARE: I am just here.

FAUST: Get out!

CARE: Why? I am in my proper place.

FAUST: (*Angry at first, then recovering himself.*)

    (No spells now...and no magic...not a trace.)

CARE: Though no listening ear can hear me,
    the inward heart will always fear me.
    On the sea and on the land,
    grim companion close at hand:
    always found, but never sought,
    flattered in word, and cursed in thought.
    Have you never met with Care?   120

FAUST: I have run up and down upon the earth:
    I grasped life's pleasures roughly, by the hair,
    exploiting everything I thought of worth.
    What I delighted in, I seized,
    relinquishing what no longer pleased,
    storming through life – at first. With age, indeed,
    I go more cautiously, and pay more heed.
    I know enough of the world, enough of men,
    to know that what's beyond's beyond our ken.
    Why need Man bother with such mysteries?   130
    What he experiences is what he is.

CARE: He whom I have in my power
    finds no pleasure from that hour.
    Eternal gloom about him lies,
    for him, suns neither set nor rise.
    His outward senses still are whole,
    but darkness now invades his soul.
    Hunger, plenty, joy and sorrow,
    he puts off until tomorrow.
    Waiting on the future, he   140
    brings nothing to maturity.

FAUST: I will not hear such folly. Go!
    Such things no wise man wants to know.

CARE: Whether he goes in or out,
    decision is submerged in doubt.
    Halfway down the road he's taken,
    he halts, and thinks he is mistaken.
    Himself and all around he hates;
    he takes a breath – and suffocates.
    Barely living, but not quitting,   150
    not despairing, not submitting.
    Whether to do or not to do?
    Which the more irksome of the two
    courses that he should pursue?
    Equally he shuns them both;
    hateful action, painful sloth.
    Crushing tension, brief release,
    uneasy sleep and troubled peace:
    these will bind him fast and well,
    and prepare his soul for Hell.   160
FAUST: Unholy spirits! This is the way that you
    have always led the human race to error.
    Even uneventful days you change into
    snares of pain, and tangled webs of terror.
    How often has poor Mankind been ensnared
    by those demons whom the early saints so feared
    when in the slothful noonday they appeared?
    Demons, I know, are hard things to defy.
    The Devil's contract's one man cannot sever.
    But, Care, your creeping power I shall deny,   170
    never acknowledge, never submit to. Never!
CARE: Then feel it now: I part from you,
    and on you one last curse I cast.
    Men are blind their whole lives through;
    so, Faust, now you be blind at last.
    (*She breathes on him.*)
FAUST: (*Blinded.*)
    Night seems to press in on me, ever more thickly;
    only the light inside my mind shines still.
    What I conceived must be fulfilled, and quickly.
    The only sovereign power is my will.

Wake up and get to work! Now! Every one of you! 180
My last great concept must be carried through.
Take up your picks and shovels! Right away!
The work's marked out, and must be done today.
Firm discipline, and diligence
attain the richest recompense.
Ruling strict and working hard
bring the final high reward.
The execution of this mighty work demands
one master spirit for a thousand hands.

4: The great forecourt of the Palace

Torches.

Enter MEPHISTOPHELES, as overseer, leading the way for a gang of LEMURES, spirits of the dead or ZOMBIES.

MEPHISTOPHELES: Come on, come in! Come on, begin!
    You shredded, patched-up creatures,
    nothing but sinews, skulls and skin,
    and vague, half-finished features.
ZOMBIES: You call – at once we are at hand,
    and as we vaguely understand,
    we stand to gain a patch of land
    that's simply lying waiting.

    The sharpened stakes are here, the wood,
    the chains, the spades, the measuring rod, 10
    but why we use such promptitude –
    Why, that we keep forgetting.
MEPHISTOPHELES: Today you won't be needing Art –
    the tallest lie down, for a start –
    now dig an oblong round about
    to hold a body of that height.
    From palace court to Man's long home;
    to this dumb end all flesh must come.
    (*ZOMBIES begin to dig with mocking gestures.*)
ZOMBIES: In youth when I did live, did love,
    methought 'twas very sweet, 20

where people sang and glasses rang,
there to direct my feet.

But Age with his stealing steps
hath clawed me in his clutch;
my feet have tumbled into the tomb,
too wide, too deep, too much.
(*FAUST comes out of the Palace, groping his way by the door-posts.*)

FAUST: The clang of pick and shovel cheers my soul.
My conscript labourers toil ceaselessly
to set the earth's new, wider boundary,
and bring the ocean under our control: 30
a limitation firm and rigorous.

MEPHISTOPHELES: (*Aside.*)
And all the time you only work for us!
While dykes and dams you still prepare,
Neptune, the sea-beast, will be there
to hold a riot unsurpassed.
No, you are damned in every sense;
we are allied to the elements,
and ruin waits for you at last.

FAUST: Overseer!

MEPHISTOPHELES: Sir!

FAUST: Use every means you can –
recruit more workers, draft every healthy man: 40
press-gang them, or, if you have to buy them,
pay what they cost. If they won't come, shanghai them.
Bring daily bulletins, which indicate
new work laid out, and current progress rate.

MEPHISTOPHELES: (*Sotto voce.*)
If what I've heard today is true,
it's not the work will be laid out – it's you.

FAUST: Along the mountain-range is all marsh ground,
infecting all that we have so far done;
to drain that festering latrine would crown
my life's work – my last triumph would be won.   50
I shall give Lebensraum to untold millions,
to live free, active lives in affluence.

Green, fertile fields, where men and herds
can live at ease upon the new-won earth,
settling on the solid, firm-set hill,
built by a bold, industrious people's skill.
Here within, a Paradise – outside,
up to the very margin, boils the tide,
gnawing its way through: when it does so, each
and every man combines to mend the breach.   60
Though there's still danger, Life and Liberty
are theirs alone who fight for them each day.
Hedged round with perils, here a man could spend
a worthy life, from childhood to the end.
I see a race grow, fearless, self-reliant,
living their lives out here, proud and defiant.
Such a race of men I long to see,
standing upon free soil, a people also free.
Then to the fleeting moment I could say:
'You are so beautiful – can you not stay?'   70
Through all of Time, the achievement of my day
upon this earth will never pass away.
I sense foreknowledge of such happiness,
and now enjoy my highest moment – this.
(*FAUST sinks back. The ZOMBIES take hold of him and lay
him out on the ground.*)
MEPHISTOPHELES: Unsatisfied by pleasure or success,
    snatching at transitory images,
    that sick and empty moment at the last
    was all the poor wretch wanted to hold fast.
    A tired old man tried to withstand
    me: now he lies stretched out there in the sand.   80
    Time wins. The clock stands still.
ZOMBIES: Midnight. No sound is heard.
    The clock-hand falls.
MEPHISTOPHELES: It falls. All is fulfilled.
ZOMBIES: All over now.
MEPHISTOPHELES: All over? What a word!
    Why so? Just gone? Pure nothing? How absurd!
    Why re-create Creation endlessly,
    simply to sweep it into vacancy?

'All over now.' What's that supposed to mean?
It is as if these things had never been;
yet the wheel turns, and re-turns, none the less.
I should prefer eternal...emptiness.   90

5: Burial

ZOMBIES: (*Solo.*)
Who was it built the house so ill,
with pickaxe and with spade?
(*Chorus.*)
For you, poor guest, in your hempen vest,
it's all too strongly made.
(*Solo.*)
Who was it furnished this sorry home,
no table and no chair?
(*Chorus.*)
It was only out on short-term loan:
creditors stripped it bare.
MEPHISTOPHELES: There lies the corpse: should the
                            soul look for ways
to escape, I'll show the bond, the blood-signed scroll.   10
But they've so many methods nowadays
to cheat the Devil of a soul.

The old procedure gives offence,
the new has not won good opinions.
I used to work alone, to all intents
and purposes. Now I rely on minions.

Nothing is going as it went before,
you can't rely on anything any more.
Time was, the soul at death would leave its house,
and – snap! – I'd catch her, like a cat and mouse.   20
But now she hesitates in the cadaver,
until the elements will no longer have her.
Death lost his grip on things some time ago:
whether he's there at all is hard to know.
I've gazed at dead limbs, hungry as a lover –
it's been a false alarm, and they'd recover.

(*With fantastic gestures of conjuration.*)
Devils of crooked and of straight-horned breed,
to me, to me, with double speed!
(*The jaws of Hell gape below, left.*)
Scare these sinners, as much as you are able;
they're all too apt to think that Hell's a fable.   30
Watch out for any phosphorescent glow,
that will be Psyche, the soul, a squalid worm
without her wings, so pull them off, and throw
her down in the centre of the fire-storm.
Make sure you grab the little pest
the moment that she leaves the nest.
(*Glory shines from above, right.*)
THE HOST OF HEAVEN: Envoys of Heaven
    float downward driven
    in unhurried flight
    sinners forgiving   40
    dead dust reviving
    traces displaying
    of your brief staying
    to all the living
    bringing delight.
MEPHISTOPHELES: That music is as irksome as that vile
    unwelcome daylight that descends on us:
    that mawkish, 'suffer-little-children' style
    beloved of the sanctimonious.
    (*ANGELS approach, scattering roses.*)
ANGELS: Roses that daze the sense   50
    scattering healing scents
    blossoms of holiness
    fires of happiness
    love they declare for you
    joy they prepare for you
    all the heart may
    to all and eternally
    gospels of charity
    show Heaven's clarity
    undying day.   60

MEPHISTOPHELES: They're coming to try to take away
my prize,
    The hypocrites – they're devils in disguise!
    I'm damned if I shall let them get away
    with this. I'll stand fast. I'm damned anyway.
    (*He regards the ANGELS, lecherously impressed.*)
ANGELS: All things at variance
    must be rejected:
    inward discordance,
    do not accept it.
    If it prove violent,
    we must prove valiant;   70
    only the loving
    are raised up by Love.
MEPHISTOPHELES: I'm burning, head, heart, liver, in
upheaval;
    this is the element of some super-devil.
    Hell's hottest fires have never burned
    as hot as this: is this why lovers snivel
    so loudly when their love is not returned?

    And now me too. What turns my head aside,
    to observe the enemy I've so long defied?
    Before, just seeing them made me wild, perverse.   80
    Has some new feeling come to light in me?
    I find them now a pleasure to the eye.
    What stops me, so I cannot even curse?

    And if *I* am made a fool of,
    who then can be called a fool?
    I hated them, and now I'm full of
    lusts that I cannot control.

    Here! Beautiful! Just tell me this – you
    must, like me, be of the race
    of Lucifer. That pretty face,   90
    frankly, makes me want to kiss you.

    I feel so natural, so at home,
    as if we'd often met before,
    so kittenish and attractive you've become,

the more I look, I am bewitched the more.
Come closer, please, give me one little look.
(*The ANGELS hover round, closing in, until the whole space
is filled with them. MEPHISTOPHELES is pressed up
against the proscenium.*)
ANGELS: We shall come closer – why do you move back?
If you are strong enough, don't move away.
MEPHISTOPHELES: You call us damned, and look at us
askance:

you are the sorcerers *par excellence.*   100
You make both men *and* women go astray.
(This is a terrible experience.
Is this the elemental power of love?
I am on fire, and yet I hardly sense
the flame that I've become the victim of.)

Come down to earth a bit: that serious style
quite suits you, but I'd love to see you smile.
Just raise the corners of your mouth; that's how
it's done – and look a bit less virtuous now.
There's too much modesty about that dress;   110
what's underneath is anybody's guess;
you could, with decency, wear rather less.
Don't turn away now! Oh! even in retreat
the rascal still looks good enough to eat.
(*Pulling himself together.*)
What happened? A sane man must, like Job, recoil
from contemplation of himself, when boil after boil
racks him, yet just that searching of his soul
will bring him triumph at the moment when
he learns trust in himself, and in his kin.

My devil's nature's reassured;   120
the dose of love was quickly cured.
Doused are the fires of temptation.
A curse on all to mark the occasion!
Mephisto is himself again.
(*The ANGELS soar up, carrying off the immortal part of
FAUST.*)

What's this? Where's the rascal gone?
You've done me, young as you may be!
The cage is open, and the bird has flown.
You little devil! You've made a fool of me.
You smuggled my prize out on the sly,
and filched my legal property.   130

Is there anyone left to hear
my suit? restore what's mine by right?
Fooled! And so late in my career,
by a fraud, and serve me right.
This whole thing has been criminally mishandled:
vast outlay, squandered shamefully; a scandal!
Dazzled by daft amours and low-down, common lust –
with my experience…! Well, it is but just.
(*Ad spectatores.*)
But if the shrewd old master chose to be
mixed up in this infantile absurdity,   140
and if in the end, it beat the Devil,
admit, it can't be all that trivial.

6: Mountain gorges – forest – cliffs – wilderness

Holy anchorites are dispersed here and there up the side of the mountain, among the rock-clefts.

CHORUS/ECHO: Forests are swaying near;
   great boulders downward bear;
   roots entangle and ensnare;
   trunks to thick trunks adhere.
   From the waves' welter
   deep caverns shelter;
   lions in dumb
   friendliness come,
   and honour the sacred shrine
   storehouse of Love divine.   10
PATER ECSTATICUS: (*Floating up and down.*)
   Rapture's eternal fire,
   bondage of pure desire,

seething pain piercing me,
God-drunken ecstasy:
arrows pursue me now,
lances subdue me now,
cudgels undo me now,
lightning's flash through me now,
so all that's worthless may
burn like a torch away   20
and one fixed star may shine
centre of Love Divine.

PATER PROFUNDUS: (*From the deep.*)
    As the chasm sheer declining
    weighs on a deeper gulf below;
    as streams in thousands frothing shining
    to the fearful smoking cataract flow;
    as great trunks forced by inward strains
    into the air erectly surge,
    so love all-powerful Demiurge
    fashions all and all sustains.   30

    The cataclysm bursts above,
    as if all Nature woke from sleep;
    the water's fullness, filled with love,
    plunges down into the deep.
    The thunderbolts that strike in fire,
    to purge the poisons from the air,
    descend in flames, with lashing rain
    ordained to irrigate the plain.

    Love's messengers the powers revealing
    which around us make and mould,   40
    may they fire my inmost feeling
    where my soul confused and cold
    in its dull sensual prison pent
    racks itself with searing pain.
    Oh God! compose my troubled brain
    bring my heart enlightenment.

PATER SERAPHICUS: (*From the Middle Regions.*)
    What is this small cloud comes gliding
    through the pine-trees' tossing hair?

Life within I sense residing;
throngs of new-made souls are there! 50
CHORUS OF THE BLESSED BOYS: Father, where is this
we hover?

Good man, tell us where we are.
We are happy to discover
that to be can be so fair!
PATER SERAPHICUS: Rise to regions ever-higher,
grow in grace invisibly:
let God's majesty inspire
and strengthen you eternally,
in the ether ruling, moulding
souls with heavenly sustenance, 60
everlasting love unfolding
into blest deliverance.
CHORUS OF THE BLESSED BOYS: Joyfully joining
spinning and wheeling
singing, entwining
in heavenly feeling,
God's word before you,
trust in His grace.
Him you adore, you
shall see face to face. 70
ANGELS: (*Floating in the upper air with the immortal part of
FAUST.*)

His spirit has been saved from ill –
our fellow-soul. Whoever
strives ceaselessly, with mind and will,
him we can deliver.

And if, over and above,
Love makes intercession,
Heaven welcomes him in Love,
wiping out transgression.
YOUNGER ANGELS: Roses, from their hands descended,
loving, holy, penitent, 80
helped our victory to cement,
and our high design was ended.

The prize of war, his soul, was ours.
As we loosed the rain of flowers,
devils fled, demons as well,
not by the usual pains of Hell
tormented, but by Love's unease.
Even Mephistopheles
was by that sharp pain undone.
Alleluja! We had won! 90
MORE PERFECT ANGELS: Still there are scraps of earth
which *we* must bear,
hindering his rebirth,
sacred and pure.

No angel may divorce
elements blended
and fused by the spirit-force.
Where two souls have ended
merged into one,
we must abide. 100
God's love alone
has power to divide.
YOUNGER ANGELS: Here, on the mountain-top,
I feel a presence,
like a cloud, mounting up
a spiritual essence.
As the clouds disappear,
I see a host move near
of children, now freed
from fetters of Earth 110
they, circling, unite.
Assuaging their need
in Heaven's rebirth
they drink in delight.
If he wishes to aspire
to a being, fuller, higher,
he must join in their flight.
CHORUS OF THE BLESSED BOYS: In joy receiving
his soul as chrysalis,

we are achieving   120
promise of Heaven's bliss.
Shake off the flakes of earth,
a last reminder!
In Heaven find rebirth
in beauty and splendour!

DOCTOR MARIANUS: (*In the highest purest cell.*)
Here the soul ranges free,
clear the horizon,
women's forms pass by me,
heavenward rising.
Ringed round with majesty,   130
star-girt in grandeur,
Queen and divinity
shown now in splendour.

Highest Empress of the Skies,
let me in the blue,
high-vaulted tent of Paradise,
pierce your mystery through.

Foster all that in Man's essence,
feelings soft and strong inspiring,
brings him near your holy presence,   140
Joy of Man's desiring.

When divinely you dictate,
nothing can withstand us.
But our fires will soon abate,
if your peace commands us.

For thee, the sinless, unabused,
power has never wanted;
thus the easily seduced
come to thee undaunted.

Highest Empress of the Earth   150
purer than all other
equal with the gods by birth
virgin sovereign mother.

By their weakness overtaken,
it is hard to save them:

unaided, few can think of breaking
those chains that enslave them.

Who can help that first quick slip
on the sloping, slippery ground?
Who is it that the eye and lip   160
of flattery does not confound?

CHORUS OF PENITENT WOMEN: Mary, Mother, dwell
                                         within us
always. Grant us, wretched sinners,
mercy, not to be withheld,
rich in love unparallelled.

MAGNA PECCATRIX: By the love that flowed in tears,
like balsam, both profound and sweet,
ignoring pharisaic jeers,
to wash Thy son, our Saviour's feet...

by the vessel full of precious   170
ointment, to those limbs applied...

by the softly flowing tresses
by which His sacred limbs were dried...

MULIER SAMARITANA: By the spring, to which were driven
Abraham's flocks in ancient days...

by the water that was given
to our Lord, his thirst to ease...

by the clear, abundant fountain,
which, since then, has flowed and streamed,
sparkling, in Grace abounding,   180
by which Mankind is redeemed...

MARIA AEGYPTIACA: By the more than hallowed tomb,
where they laid Our Lord in mourning...

by the strong immortal arm
that thrust the sinner back in warning...

by the forty years' repentance
lived out in the desert land...

by the final, dying sentence
traced in farewell in the sand...

THE THREE: Even from the greatly sinning   190
You do not avert your gaze,

Grant to us, repentant women,
An eternity of days.
You, who pardon all transgression,
do not turn away your face:
grant this soul, though fallen from grace,
your divinest intercession.

UNA POENITENTIUM: (*Once known as GRETCHEN,*
coming in closer.)

Look down, look down,
Thou rich in Heaven's crown,
pattern of all renown,   200
look kindly on my happiness;
the earthly lover,
all torments over,
returns in bliss.

CHORUS OF BLESSED BOYS: (*Flying nearer in circles.*)

Powerful of limb
he rises above:
our care of him
repaying in Love.
We could not live for long
with earthly creatures.   210
This man has learned Life's song –
now he will teach us.

THE PENITENT: (*Once known as GRETCHEN.*)

Surrounded by the spirit-choir,
spirit himself, with other spirits,
the stranger-soul is scarce aware
of the new life that he inherits.
See! how from every bond of earth
he tears the shackles of the past;
from heavenly garments of rebirth
he steps in youth and strength at last!   220
Let me teach him, let me guide him,
still dazzled by the new-sprung day.

MATER GLORIOSA: To the highest sphere now lead him;
knowing you, he knows the way.

DOCTOR MARIANUS: (*Prostrate in adoration.*)
    Gaze in penitence on the eyes
    and image of salvation;
    and in gratitude arise
    to beatification.
    Virgin, Mother, Goddess, Queen;
    in Thy service now be seen   230
    every sanctified endeavour.
    Keep us in Thy Grace forever.
CHORUS MYSTICUS: All that shall pass away
    is but reflection.
    All insufficiency
    here finds perfection.
    All that's mysterious
    here finds the day.
    Woman in all of us
    shows us our way.   240

The End.